"David M. Edwards gives us the practical and insightful steps to draw closer to God. Easily understood, simply presented, *Encountering God* is David's best work yet."

Margaret Becker, singer and songwriter

"Knowing David Edwards's heart and writing skills, I was eager to read what I expected to be a gem of a book. But I found instead *many* gems—each chapter a priceless insight into how God proactively seeks to engage us in an intimate and powerful love relationship. I finished the book only to begin reading it immediately again and plan to put it on my read-it-once-a-year shelf."

Kenn Gulliksen, pastor and founder, Vineyard Movement

"*Encountering God* beckons the reader to embark upon a journey, one that is masterfully guided by the storytelling hand of author David M. Edwards."

from the foreword by **Julie Reid**, executive editor, *Worship Leader* magazine

ENCOUNTERING
GOD

ENCOUNTERING GOD

10 Ways to
Experience His Presence

DAVID M. EDWARDS

BakerBooks
a division of Baker Publishing Group
Grand Rapids, Michigan

Published by Baker Books
a division of Baker Publishing Group
P.O. Box 6287, Grand Rapids, MI 49516-6287
www.bakerbooks.com

Printed in the United States of America

Library of Congress Cataloging-in-Publication Data
Edwards, David M., pastor.
    Encountering God : 10 ways to experience His presence / David M. Edwards.
        p.   cm.
    ISBN 978-0-8010-6832-4 (pbk.)
    1. Presence of God. 2. Presence of God—Biblical teaching. 3. Bible—Criticism, interpretation, etc. I. Title.
BT180.P6E39 2008
248.4—dc22   2007047276

This book is published in association with the literary agency of Sanford Communications, Inc., 16778 S.E. Cohiba Ct., Damascus, OR 97089.

In keeping with biblical principles of creation stewardship, Baker Publishing Group advocates the responsible use of our natural resources. As a member of the Green Press Initiative, our company uses recycled paper when possible. The text paper of this book is comprised of 30% post-consumer waste.

This book is dedicated to Susan.

Let nothing make thee sad or fretful,
Or too regretful,
Be still;
What God hath ordered must be right,
Then find in it thine own delight,
My will.
Why shouldst thou fill today with sorrow
About tomorrow,
My heart?
One watches all with care most true,
Doubt not that He will give thee too
Thy part.
Only be steadfast, never waver,
Nor seek earth's favour,
But rest:
Thou knowest what God wills must be
For all His creatures, so for thee,
The best.

                    Paul Flemming, 1609–1640

CONTENTS

Contents

FOREWORD

An amazing phenomenon occurs in New York City during United Nations week. Manhattan bustles with activity like no other time during the year. Picture foreign dignitaries, Secret Service men everywhere, and a sea of black Lincoln Town Cars.

At the very least, your curiosity is piqued; you can't help but wonder who will step out of the next caravan that pulls up. People literally stop on the street, peering into the impenetrably tinted windows. Many of the main streets are closed, and police officers are stationed on every corner to offer protection and directions to the onlookers and passersby.

I recently had the opportunity to experience United Nations week firsthand. Our cab driver warned us that it would be difficult to get around town, to get into restaurants, and to get out of town via the local airport. Surrounding the United Nations building, the streets were teeming with people hoping to have a "chance encounter" with one of these foreign dignitaries and figureheads called on to participate in the Global Peace Initiative. I have to admit, even I snuck past a couple of security personnel in hope of catching a glimpse of someone I might recognize.

Having just finished reading *Encountering God*, I couldn't help but notice the irony as I was running around the streets of New York City, working hard to meet strangers who were working equally hard to avoid contact with me (or anyone for that matter). Contrast that with our God, who delights in meeting with His people. As it says in Zephaniah 3:17 (NIV), "The LORD your God is with you, he is mighty to save. He will take great delight in you, he will quiet you with his love, he will rejoice over you with singing." Not only is He with us, He delights in His people.

God's love and availability are the soul of *Encountering God*, and there is no better time for us to hear this message. Edwards uses his adept hand to bring the majesty of God into an intimate connection with His people. A God who is far above anything we can dream or perceive yet knows the number of times you have taken a breath.

Luke 15:4 says that our Lord will leave the many who are found to search for the one who is lost. Edwards helps us find that it is the nature of God's character—His divine drive—to actually pursue us because of His love for us.

Maybe you find yourself in a place today where you are chasing after something that eludes you. But God isn't that fleeing stranger; He wants to be found by us.

The Word says in Jeremiah 29:13 (NIV) that "you will seek me and find me when you seek me with all your heart." Think about that for a minute: God wants to be found by you, and He delights in His time with you. Isn't that refreshing?

Some of us are faced with nervousness when we consider the implications of having an encounter with God. The very thought of coming into the presence of a Holy God means that there is bound to be power— even radical transformation. As we spend time in the Word, we can't help but be surprised by the outcomes of the many encounters between God and His people throughout history.

Encountering God beckons the reader to embark upon a journey, one that is masterfully guided by the storytelling hand of author David M. Edwards. The journey is broken into ten touch points in time, and we are able to lay our burdens down and move through a book that is both well written and shines the light into the areas of our lives that are desperately in need of it. What an amazing service Edwards offers us. He truly writes with a heart for the individuals who share his journey. And he takes a further step to interact with readers and invite them to engage through questions that will move you closer to that place where you can encounter God today.

With a fresh eye on our oldest texts, Edwards brings to light people like Moses, who received a glimpse of God's glory and a nation was freed forever; Abraham, who received a promise and an inheritance for multiple generations; the woman who reached out in faith, touched the hem of Jesus's garment, and was healed—and her desperate actions embolden us to do the same; Mary, who received a place in history by sparing no expense, showing us all how to kneel before our Lord. Then Edwards dares to ask us, How might your life be transformed by an encounter with God today?

Worship leader, author, pastor, recording artist, and editor of *The Worshiper* magazine, David M. Edwards has a gift for taking what is oftentimes a difficult, and even intimidating, subject—that of worship—and making it approachable for the person who needs to understand it the most: the worshiper. What a joy it is to delve into this book and read both practical theology and enjoyable storytelling, along with questions that are thought provoking.

This book is suited for everyone—whether prone to journeying into deeper waters or content with skipping along the surface—to glean significant insights into your personal spiritual life and journey. Each of the ten encounters that Edwards explores allows the examination of a variety of topics, helping the reader expand their understanding of worship from a new vantage point.

As you read on, you will be invited to encounter God, a frightening yet wonderful gift from an inspired writer, pastor, and friend.

Julie Reid, executive editor
Worship Leader magazine

ACKNOWLEDGMENTS

I would be remiss not to mention the following people with whom God has blessed and enriched my life. We are all products of our environment to a great degree, and I am grateful for the environment the Lord has created around me with such wonderfully skilled and gifted people who share my passion and have taught me much about encountering God. I am forever in their debt.

I wish to express my sincere appreciation to Chad Allen and everyone at Baker for their support and belief in this project and in the calling God has placed on my life.

To my literary agent, David Sanford, and the entire staff at Sanford Communications, Inc., thank you so much for your guidance and perseverance. A very special thank-you goes to Elizabeth Jones for her editing skills and putting up with me.

To my manager, Glenda J. McNalley, there is no finer manager in the business or truer friend. We have walked many a mile and many more still lie ahead. Thank you for your wisdom, insight, and guidance.

To my beautiful wife, Susan, thank you for your love and support that continue to give me strength. I love you!

To Tara, Elyse, and Evan, Daddy loves you so much, and I am so very proud of you all and what God is doing in your lives.

To my parents, Louis and Wanda Edwards, you are the greatest parents in all the world. Thank you for everything!

To my brother, Daniel, thank you for always being a faithful friend.

To Julie Reid for endless phone calls, emails, and thinking out loud with me about our favorite topic: worship! Your love and friendship mean so much to us.

To Dr. Chuck Fromm, thank you for giving me a place to serve and the freedom to create. Thanks for not being afraid to push the envelope open as wide as possible!

And for a multitude of reasons: Craig Adams, Joe Beck, Margaret Becker, Regi Stone, Andraé Crouch, Dr. Jack Hayford, Kim Hill, Daniele Kimes, Sue Olson, Dr. Herbert Prince, Caleb Quaye, Denise Robinson, Harlan Rogers, Alan Shacklock, Phil Sillas, and Rich and Erica Usher.

INTRODUCTION

People are hungry for an encounter with God. They are constantly trying to fill the void within—that deep hunger for the Holy. And yet the God-shaped void within each of us was and is made to accommodate only the Lord God, Jehovah, Creator of the ends of the earth. Trouble, frustration, unsettledness, and constant doubt haunt our lives when we try to fill the void with anything other than Him.

Remember when the children of Israel were just beginning to trek out over the desert after their deliverance from Egypt? The Bible tells us that God's Presence appeared to them as a pillar of cloud by day and a pillar of fire by night. Whenever the "cloud" moved, the people moved as well. My life has taught me that God won't allow me to sit still very long, and when He decides to move, I'd better follow or I will be stuck in the desert! Just when you think it's time to sit back and relax, proud of all you have "accomplished,"

God decides it's time for you to go and learn something new.

For me, each one of these times—of learning, of testing, of endurance, of perseverance, of abiding—is a new and fresh encounter with the God who loves me and gave His one and only Son to die for my sin. The entire Bible is one grand epic describing humanity's quest for an encounter with God and God's desire to encounter His people, both corporately and individually. God wants to encounter, engage, intersect, intervene, show up, even startle us with His Presence. And His Word provides ample evidence that He can and will show up just about anywhere and sometimes when you least expect Him.

While the Bible is filled with stories of encounters with God, I've chosen ten that have personally touched my life, and I've tried to synthesize them here through the grid of my own experience. They're like ten touchstones that can open us up to a fresh encounter with the living God. If we take to heart the lessons they teach and become "doers" of the Word, I believe we will find ourselves in a place of fresh understanding of God's promises, God's power, and God's provision.

These stories have changed my worship, enhanced my praise, called me to surrender, and bolstered my faith. Join me in discovering how we can encounter God afresh, as ten brothers and sisters in the Bible did, by pouring out our life, cleaning house, rejoicing in the Lord always, building an altar of uncut stone, reaching out for Jesus, building a memorial with our life, trusting in His name, offering sacrifices of praise, always thanking Him, and making the ultimate sacrifice of self.

These aren't one-off experiences—after you've done each one once, you move on and that's it. Rather, these "spiritual exercises" grow in their importance and impact as you revisit them time and again throughout your walk with the Lord. Learning from people who walked in faith before us has taught me the timelessness of their testimony. For as much as this world has changed, we as people have not changed at all in our need for love, acceptance, and forgiveness—our need for God.

Tragic news continues to splash across the headlines of the Internet and television. These are the telltale signs of a people who need an encounter with the living God. If every person who claimed to be a Christian would pursue God as much as God pursues him or her, our collective encounters with Him would so change our lives that we would make people hungry for His presence just by our being around them. The Bible tells us, "Taste and see that the LORD is good" (Ps. 34:8). One taste, one encounter with the Lord of life, ruins anyone for anything else!

God has chosen to make Himself accessible to people. This happens in salvation, through Jesus Christ, in the dwelling of the Holy Spirit within the believer, and when we worship Him. He has chosen to inhabit our praise and make His presence known. God wants to spend time with you and me. He longs to be a part of every second of every day. I encourage you to invite Him into every aspect of your life. Let

His Word penetrate your heart and mind, changing you and making you clean.

Let's pray as we begin to journey through this book.

Dear Lord Jesus,

You have promised to fill those who hunger and thirst after righteousness. You have promised to give to those who ask, open the door to those who knock, and to those who seek, You said they would find. I am hungry for You. I need You now more than ever. I am in a place of asking, seeking, and knocking, because I desire for a fresh encounter with You. I am tired of being in the same place and not going anywhere. Even now, I recognize that the "cloud" of Your Presence is getting ready to move, and I want to move with it. I thank You for loving me and for all that You have done for me, but I want more of You. I'm not here to seek Your hands, but Your face—Your Presence. By Your Holy Spirit, lead me and guide me in all truth and righteousness and set me free to be the person You have called and created me to be.

In Your powerful Name I ask these things.

Amen.

1

POUR OUT YOUR LIFE

Finding the Courage
to Put the Cause before the Cost

Mark 14:3–9; John 12:1–8

I have very fond memories of times spent with family and friends—especially those who have passed on and are now with the Lord. When I was young, I had two wonderful grandmothers, both Christians who loved Jesus very much.

In the winter my grandmothers wore coats with big fur collars. When they hugged me, my nose would stick right into the fur collar, and it always smelled like walking through a perfume factory. Their favorite perfume had collected in that fur collar over the years, and it wasn't going anywhere soon!

My cousins and I made fun of the smell, but today whenever I catch a whiff of their perfume or even something similar, I smile as my mind runs back to my grandmas hugging me and my little face getting buried in their coats. I love that smell; I wouldn't trade anything for the comforting memories it brings me.

Keep reading for a story about a different smell, even more precious than my grandmas' perfume, an aroma that lingers in the air to this very day.

Breaking the Seal

It was springtime in Palestine—six days before Passover. Jesus, one week away from His crucifixion, arrived in the small village of Bethany on the outskirts of Jerusalem. There He spent an evening with some of His closest friends. Among them were Lazarus, Martha, and Mary—three siblings who were followers of our Lord. A week earlier Lazarus had been sick and died, but Jesus raised him to life again, so at this gathering they must have had quite a conversation!

Sometime following the evening meal, Mary brought out an alabaster box, which contained spikenard, a wonderful, fragrant, and very expensive oil imported from India. The oil that Mary had was worth a whole year's wages.

Breaking the seal on the alabaster box, she bowed before the Lord Jesus and poured the oil on His feet. As she poured, the oil must have run in and around every groove and muscle of each foot. It would have flowed between His toes and down His heels to the soles of His feet, all the while washing away the dirt, dust, and stench of earth. After anointing His feet, she wiped them with her hair. As she performed this act of sacrificial, loving worship, the Bible says that the entire house was filled with the fragrance of the costly perfume.

I want to have that fragrance of worship in my house! I want that fragrance of surrender to permeate everything I do and to have that sweet perfume released in my life again and again as I fall at Jesus's feet and worship Him. Loving Jesus must be my first priority. I long to be broken and spilled out at His feet just like that perfume.

> Only the heart knows how to find what is precious.
>
> Fyodor Dostoyevsky

Taking the Opportunity

When you do something for the Lord, you will usually experience some resistance. It comes in many different forms, but it all has the same source: the devil. Sometimes it's a voice in your head that second-guesses you, judges you, makes fun of you, or makes light of your service to the King. But the devil is a liar and the father of lies!

The Gospel of John tells us that Judas Iscariot complained about the cost of Mary's sacrifice, that it should have been used to help the poor, but his concern was anything but sincere. Judas was dipping into the till! Here was Judas going on about the price of Mary's worship when he couldn't have cared less about the poor.

Jesus responded, "The poor you have with you always, but Me you do not have always" (John 12:8). Jesus's comments about the poor simply meant this: service that will have no other opportunity must take preference over perpetual or ongoing duties. Can you imagine if Mary had missed this opportunity? Had she been saving the precious oil for such a time as this? What if she had given in to the thought, *Oh, I don't feel like doing it now. I'll do it next week*? As it turns out, "next week" would have been too late.

How many times have I missed out on an opportunity to encounter the Lord because I was too busy doing other things? How many instances have there been when it could have been just the Lord and me, but I went off to do something else? How many times have I been in a worship service, yet the worship service wasn't in me?

Mary's sacrifice reminds us that if we want to do something for Jesus, we shouldn't wait.

Love is loveliest when embalmed in tears.

Sir Walter Scott

The Lingering Fragrance of a Poured-Out Life

In Mark's account of the story, he adds something Jesus said that is so significant to the event: "Assuredly,

I say to you, wherever this gospel is preached throughout the whole world, what this woman did will also be spoken of as a memorial to her" (14:9).

Think about it. Here I am today writing about what happened in this home two thousand years ago! Jesus was right. Even more important than the recorded history of the event is *the lingering effect of a poured-out life*!

The lingering effect of Mary's poured-out life makes me long to offer that same sacrificial worship. Though I do not smell spikenard, I smell worship, sacrifice, brokenness, a poured-out life, an attitude that believes no cost is too great if it's for the Lord Jesus Christ.

When someone dies, it is not unusual for a friend or relative to pick up an article of clothing or other personal effect and notice the loved one's scent still on it. Her perfume or his cologne seems to linger to comfort us. Then there are flowers and foods and plants that remind us of happy times with that person. One smell can transport us back in time. People who live a broken and poured-out life leave behind the aroma of worship.

You see, *sacrifice for the sake of Jesus will have a perpetual influence*. When my children are in a difficult situation, I want them to remember what I would have done and be influenced to do the same. I want to lay a godly foundation in my home that will influence my kids long after I'm gone. I want them to remember the fragrance being poured out before the Lord, the fragrance of worship, sacrifice, and total submission to God.

We've all had people do us wrong—and we always will—but rather than creating a stumbling block for others, we ought to get down on our hands and knees and break open the alabaster box and pour it all out before the Lord. Rather than be bitter, why don't we worship and be better? Rather than leave the stench of jealousy and hard-heartedness, why don't we leave the fragrance of faithfulness? Then when our family and friends are facing tough situations, the sweet smell of our prayers and worship will come back to them.

> Sacrifice for the sake of Jesus will have a perpetual influence.

The sacrifices of God are a broken spirit, a broken and a contrite heart—these, O God, You will not despise.

Psalm 51:17

In our own lives we pay taxes, but we give gifts; we show up for work because we're obligated, but we volunteer at church because we want to. We give our time and resources to things that matter to us—things that strike a chord within, that touch our hearts and move us with compassion. We do it because we want to, not because we're forced to. We quickly learn that we receive far more pleasure and joy from giving than from getting.

Mary presented a precious gift to Jesus not out of duty but out of the goodness of her heart. Jesus didn't demand it or seek it. Its giving was simply an act of worship.

How important this is! We should all seek to worship God from a place where the posture of our heart is one of simply wanting to lavish on Him the love, glory, and honor that He deserves.

Ministry *to* Jesus

Lazarus, Martha, and Mary all loved Jesus very much, but only one of them anointed His feet. Only one of them spent a year's wages to worship Him. Lazarus sat beside Jesus at the table. Martha was busy in the kitchen. Only Mary bowed at His feet, broke the seal on the alabaster box, and poured out the oil. Why didn't Lazarus jump up and do the same? Why didn't Martha stop what she was doing and join Mary?

Here we have a picture of the church. Many people are willing to sit beside Jesus and trust in Him for their salvation, but they do little else. Then there are those who are so busy doing church work, they don't have time to pray or read their Bible. They find it hard to stop to worship and spend time with the Lord. Finally, there are those who know that our ministry *to* Jesus must come before our ministry *for* Jesus.

Our ministry to Jesus has a strong impact on what we can do for Him. We won't have that much to give away if we're not taking anything in. If we're not spending time bowing before Jesus, how can we stand before people? When was the last time we took a good look at His feet? When was the last time we lavished our love on the Lord? He is thrilled when you involve yourself in ministry and volunteer for this and that—it's part of your spiritual responsibility and development as a believer. But He longs for you to just love Him the way Mary did.

The strength to stand for Jesus is found in pouring our life out at His feet. The strength to do great things for God is found in giving Him our all. The strength to shape nations and cities is first found in some willing vessel pouring his or her life out at the feet of Jesus. In loving surrender we spend everything we have for one moment at His feet.

The cause is greater than the cost. I want to empty myself before Him. When people are around me, I want them to be able to say, "What is that pleasing aroma? It must be the aroma of worship; it must be the aroma of sacrifice; it must be the aroma of total submission; it must be the aroma of being broken and poured out."

What would cause Mary to spend an entire year's wages on one act of worship? Through her story, we can see the culmination of a life poured out in selfless homage to a Savior who was days away from pouring out His life for all. There is no price too high to honor the One who was willing to pay for our salvation with His blood. The fragrance of her sacrifice lingered long after the costly perfume had been used up. And so it is with our lives—the fragrance of a poured-out life will linger long after we're gone. Our acts of sacrifice and worship now can serve as guideposts to encourage others to serve and worship God.

Do not look for God in any particular way, but look
for Him.

Oswald Chambers

Broken and Poured Out

Like Mary's gift, Jesus was broken and poured out
for you and me. Isaiah 53:12 says, "Therefore I will
divide Him a portion with the great, and He shall
divide the spoil with the strong, because He poured
out His soul unto death, and He was numbered with
the transgressors, and He bore the sin of many, and
made intercession for the transgressors."

I was one of the transgressors for whom He made
intercession. I was one of the sinners for whom He
poured out His soul unto death. Jesus was broken and
poured out. He spilled His own blood on the cross to
save us, and the lingering effects of His poured-out
life are still saving people today! The sweet fragrance
of the cross fills anyone who comes to Him.

Jesus said, "Take, eat; this is My body which is
broken for you," and "This cup is the new covenant
in My blood" (1 Cor. 11:24–25). He was broken and
poured out.

When I first came to Jesus, I knelt down, and through
the air came a fragrance that was familiar to me. I had
smelled that fragrance before around my parents and
grandparents. I had smelled that fragrance every week
in our church as people prayed and sang of God's love,
mercy, and grace, and when God's glory showed up.

And on my knees, there it was again, that smell, that fragrance, that sweet perfume still filling the earth. It was the smell of worship, sacrifice, submission. It was the smell of being broken and spilled out, and now it was my turn to pour out my life, my will, my wants, my ways, and say, "Lord, I gladly pour everything that I am before You in loving surrender."

Isn't that what being a Christian is all about? It's the desire to be more and more like Jesus. We are to be imitators of Christ and, like Him, live lives that are poured out in loving service to our King. May each of us find the courage to put the cause before the cost.

Encountering God Today

1. The worship of Mary of Bethany reminds us that the cause is greater than the cost. Because she was a worshiper at heart, she spared no expense in lavishing her gift on the Lord Jesus. Why is it important for us to remember that Jesus is more important than anything else in the entire world?

2. Pouring our life out for God involves more than just one act of worship. However, Mary's one act of worship recorded in the Bible communicates clearly that worship is a lifestyle. What are your acts of worship? Is worship a lifestyle for you? What can you learn from Mary's story?

3. Why is it so important to minister to Jesus first before ministering to others? Can you think of a time when you tried to minister to others when you had nothing to give?

4. Jesus poured His life out for our sins. He told us to pick up our cross and follow Him. What are ways in which we can pour out our lives for the Lord? What can we learn from His selfless example?

2

CLEAN HOUSE

Coming Back to a Tender Heart

2 Kings 22:1–20; 23:1–25

Have you ever been digging through the basement, the garage, or a drawer, when all of a sudden you come across something that you haven't seen in a while? You begin to wonder just how long it has been missing, but you're equally puzzled by the reality that you didn't know it was misplaced! Like a kid with a secret or a hidden treasure, maybe you stop what you're doing and proudly take the item to someplace safe and secure just in case it decides to wander off again.

Whenever this happens to me, I always try to analyze the how and when of the situation—knowing very well that it had to have been me who misplaced the item. This teaches me that in the everydayness of life, stuff gets pushed aside, not intentionally, but just because. With many items and various paraphernalia cluttering our desks, nightstands, cupboards, and lives, a once-treasured belonging, no longer in our line of sight, can be forgotten as other things move in and fill up the empty space.

People often say, "You don't know what you've got 'til it's gone." I guess that can be true, but what about someone who never knew they had it to begin with? My grandparents had an ancient Indian burial ground underneath their home, and for years they never knew it. It wasn't until they decided to dig out a cellar that they came across it. They contacted the state university concerning their find, and the university was ecstatic that my grandparents wanted to donate the contents of the site to them. The university studied the bones, pottery, and jewelry from the site and then proudly put them on display. Here was something of great value within my grandparents' reach, but they never knew it. Sometimes we don't realize what is around us until a series of events opens our eyes.

In the middle of difficulty lies opportunity.

Albert Einstein

34

A Heart after God

The year was 640 BC, and Judah had a new king on the throne, Josiah. King Josiah was only eight years old when his father, King Amon, was assassinated, and Josiah ascended the throne. Josiah's father and grandfather, King Manasseh, had done evil in the sight of God. They allowed altars to false gods to be set up in the temple of the Lord God of Israel and allowed divination and witchcraft to be practiced there. Although Manasseh repented before he died, it was too little too late, and it did not effect a positive spiritual change for the nation. Thus young Josiah inherited a nation that practiced witchcraft, idolatry, child sacrifices to demon gods, astrology, and every kind of wickedness imaginable. God's judgment was certainly imminent. However, Josiah, unlike his father and grandfather, had a heart after God.

In his twenty-sixth year of life, King Josiah ordered Hilkiah, the high priest, to restore the temple of God. Although tithes and offerings were obviously being received, they were not being spent on what God intended: to care for the needs of the priests, the work of the ministry, and the upkeep and repairs of the temple. So Josiah commanded Hilkiah to distribute the tithes and offerings properly so that the temple and the ministry, for which it was built, would be restored. As they began to restore and clean up the temple, Hilkiah came across the book of the Law, or the book of Moses, which was the Pentateuch—the first five books of the Bible. Though within reach, it had been missing for a very long time.

Quickly Hilkiah and a scribe named Shaphan reported to King Josiah what had been found, and the king had the book read to him. On hearing the Word of the Lord, Josiah tore his clothes as a sign of deep godly sorrow because the people were living so contrary to God's will and Word. Immediately, with great repentance and remorse, Josiah asked Hilkiah to seek the Lord on his and the people's behalf to see what they should do. The high priest sought out Huldah, a prophetess of the Lord God.

After hearing their report and the sequence of events, Huldah began to prophesy God's will to them and directed the following words to Josiah: "Because your heart was tender, and you humbled yourself before the LORD . . . and [because] you tore your clothes and wept before Me, I also have heard you" (2 Kings 22:19).

When King Josiah heard the prophetic word from Huldah, he sent for all the elders of Judah to meet him at the temple. All the people of Jerusalem came as well to hear what the king was going to say. Josiah had the contents of the book of the law read aloud to the people so that everyone could hear the Word of the Lord. King Josiah was essentially calling the people to repent of their sins so that they could experience a spiritual restoration and not just a restoration of a physical structure—the temple. Josiah was getting ready to rout the enemy.

Then the king made a public covenant before the Lord. He promised to follow His will and His Word with all his heart and soul. He commanded Hilkiah to clean house! It was time to clean out the temple. It was time for a religious purge, ridding the house of God of every unsanctified object, every shrine, every altar to Baal, Asherah, or Molech, as well as the opportunity to practice all manner of sexual perversion in honor of these demon gods, including human sacrifice, which was required by the religion of Molech.

This seems unbelievable, and yet it shows us the progression of sin and how one sin leads to another, which leads to another, until people are so desensitized to the voice and Word of God that literally an "anything goes" policy is adopted by all. One can only imagine how the heart of God must have grieved over this. The very people who were recipients of his blessing and promise had cast the God of heaven and all creation aside for some impotent handmade deity that you could step on and break! Absurd, and yet how like our own society today. Sin hasn't changed all that much, and the devil uses the same tactics to draw our hearts away from the truth.

When Josiah gave the order to clean the house, I am sure that those involved in all the sinful practices didn't go quietly, but they did have to go because the king said so. As they dragged both people and sacrilegious objects out into the glaring light of day, it had to have raised more than a few eyebrows! I'm sure the king and others were speechless, and the overwhelming sense of guilt and remorse must have flooded over the city that day as their sin was put on parade. As the cleaning went on, word began to spread that it was a new day in Jerusalem.

How Things Turned Around

Let's look again at the elements of this momentous spiritual occasion and see what the Lord has to say to us.

The Past Doesn't Have to Be the Future

Josiah came from bad stock. His heritage certainly worked against him. He was fatherless at eight years old, and his father and grandfather had allowed every form of idolatry, witchcraft, and perverted sex acts to take place before the altar of God. This would be like a Christian church building making room for a statue of Buddha, a Hindu shrine, a pentagram in the floor, and temple prostitutes.

But Josiah didn't look for sympathy when he found things so contrary to God's Word; he looked to God. He made the right choice. God broke the family curse that was on him and blessed Josiah because he honored the Lord.

No matter what your past or where you come from or how little you had or how bad it was, you don't have to be like your past, act like your past, or live in your past. Jesus came to set the captives free. Jesus came to reverse the curse. Let Him reverse it in you as He did in Josiah.

It is never too late to be what you might have been.

George Eliot

The Bible Was Lost in the Temple

It is truly astonishing that Hilkiah found the book of the law that had been lost, right in the temple. Can you imagine a church without a Bible? Well, here's one for you—right in our text. How long had the book of the law been missing? Obviously for some time, given the behavior of the people and the desecration of the temple that had gone on for at least sixty years. The temple of God had no Word of God for sixty years! A likely scenario is that someone (such as a priest) who cared very much about God's Word was concerned the holy book would be destroyed during the idolatrous reigns of Manasseh and Amon, so he hid it. No doubt this was one of the earliest copies of God's Word.

Another thing to consider is that this discovery bears witness to God's guiding and controlling hand, guarding His inspired Word and protecting it from destruction by idolaters and apostates; indeed, the inspired written Word of God is indestructible: "The grass withers, the flower fades, but the word of our God stands forever" (Isa. 40:8).

The story of Hilkiah's finding the Word of God shows us that it's possible to go to church year after year after year and never change. It's not enough to show up at church because it seems like the right thing to do. Remember: "Faith comes by hearing, and hearing by the word of God" (Rom. 11:17). You have to have a relationship with God for change to come to your life. And to have a relationship with God, you need to know His Word and allow the Word to work within your heart and life (see Prov. 4:20–23).

You Don't Have to Be a Pastor for God to Use You

The prophet Joel said, "And it shall come to pass afterward that I will pour out My Spirit on all flesh; your sons and your daughters shall prophesy . . . ; on My menservants and on My maidservants I will pour out My Spirit in those days" (Joel 2:28–29). Although his prophecy took place two hundred years after Josiah, we can see little glimpses of it here in the life of Huldah the prophetess. We find that God is no respecter of persons when it comes to ministry. He will use anyone who's humble and willing to be a vessel for Him.

> God is no respecter of persons when it comes to ministry. He will use anyone who's humble and willing to be a vessel for Him.

Even as God didn't think twice about establishing Deborah as a judge in Israel, He uses a woman here who is able to hear the Word of God and interpret it with the help of the Holy Spirit. I just love the fact that the king asks the high priest to inquire of the Lord on his behalf. Instead of the high priest's doing it himself, he runs to Huldah, who obviously has a positive track record of ministry and is respected for her relationship with God.

She is not the high priest, and yet she is the one God uses to deliver His Word to the king and the people of Judah. You don't have to be the pastor for God to use you. You just have to be ready and willing. Huldah's prophecy sparked one of the greatest revivals in the history of God's people.

May each of us have such a positive spiritual track record that God would be able to send people our way for words of encouragement and comfort. Like Huldah, may we earn the respect of those around us as people who take their relationship with the Lord seriously.

A Tender Heart Will Always Gain God's Attention

The second half of Huldah's prophecy is directed to Josiah (see 2 Kings 23:19). It contains some of the tenderest language that God has spoken to anyone. In it we discover the secret to Josiah's success and the apparent blessing on his life.

Because your heart was tender . . .

God does not reveal His secrets to people who are full of themselves or who think they have all of the answers. God reveals Himself to the broken and the spent, to those who pour themselves out before Him and sincerely say, "Lord, give me a tender heart."

And you humbled yourself . . .

We will never get anywhere with God until we learn to humble ourselves before Him. We need to get down on our knees and admit that we cannot do it by ourselves and that we must have His help in our lives. When we worship Him and not people, confess our sins and repent, and forgive others, we are living humbly before the Lord, and He will raise us up. Neither you nor I will ever receive God's grace or be renewed without first humbling ourselves.

You tore your clothes and wept before Me, I also have heard you . . .

It's interesting to note that neither tearing your clothes nor weeping is considered verbal communication; however, God said that when Josiah did those things, God *heard* him! God understands every tear and every sigh. God understands why you do what you do and why you don't do what you don't do. God looks at the heart. He knows what you're going to say even when *you* don't. I'm so thankful for a loving God who knows me inside and out. He understands me like no other.

The People Took a Stand for the Covenant

When the king made a public covenant before the Lord, he promised to follow God's will and His Word with all his heart and soul. Then we are told something so significant and indeed crucial to the beginning of the coming revival: "And all the people took their stand for the covenant" (2 Kings 23:3).

To *take a stand* means to agree with the covenant—which was the Word of God. After hearing God's holy Word, the people's collective response was, "Yes, we all agree!" When people walk and live in agreement with God's Word, a measure of blessing comes on their life because God always honors His Word and blesses those who obey it. We are called to "do" the Word—not just "hear" it (James 1:22). If revival and restoration are to come in untold measure, repentance among the people must come first. Then the people must take a stand—an agreement that God's Word should be obeyed, followed, sought after, hungered for, revered, and honored.

> The men who stand straightest in the presence of sin, bow lowest in the presence of God.
>
> F. B. Meyer

Clean the House

Josiah was determined to eliminate idolatry if it was the last thing he did. He commanded the high priest, Hilkiah, to clean the house. As the temple was cleansed, the degree of degradation and evil was almost unbelievable. They brought out idols and carved images to other gods, idolatrous priests that served and channeled these demons, male prostitutes that were having sex in the temple of Jehovah, astrologers, and those who were responsible for sacrificing children to Molech, among other detestable things.

Josiah destroyed the altars on the roof of the temple that were used to worship the planets and stars. He destroyed the altars that were built to worship Baal, Asherah, Ashtoreth, Milcom, Chemosh, and Molech. And then Josiah began to go into the countryside and destroy the evil shrines there as well.

It seems incomprehensible that the people to whom God commanded, "You shall have no other gods before Me," had allowed this stuff to go on and willingly participated in such perverse evil. On the outside, the temple might have appeared somewhat intact, but inside it was full of corruption.

If we're going to live for God, we're going to have to go all the way in our commitment. We must rid ourselves of everything alien to the revealed will of God. The Bible tells us plainly that God no longer lives in temples or tabernacles, but through His Holy Spirit He lives in temples of flesh: "Do you not know that you are the temple of God and that the Spirit of God dwells in you?" (1 Cor. 3:16). We are the temples in which God dwells. He lives in the house of our heart.

If we were to look inside our own temple, we might not see a recognizable idol or statue. Rarely do we look at our spiritual life and see a big statue with the word *idol* emblazoned on it. But it's important to investigate what is in our temple. What is in your heart? Are there vestiges of the past that need to be cleaned out? If you were to take a good look, would you find unconfessed sin, ungodly habits, resentment, unforgiveness, jealousy, secret fantasies about someone else's spouse, and other sins? What is in there? If we are to be free and clean, all of this must come out.

We have to clean house! We can't call the high priest, as King Josiah did, to do the cleaning. You and I must be the ones to personally remove the toxic thoughts, attitudes, and actions. Once removed through confession and repentance, there's only one cleaning agent known to humankind to remove the stain: *the blood of Jesus!*

Keep the Passover

After cleaning out the temple, Josiah killed the pagan priests and burned their bones on the very demonic altars where they had served. Then he addressed the people, saying to them, "Keep the Passover to the Lᴏʀᴅ your God, as it is written in this Book of the Covenant" (2 Kings 23:21).

Through the power of the Holy Spirit, the king was essentially saying, "It's great that we have cleaned out the temple and destroyed idolatry, but that's only the beginning. We must now commit ourselves all the way and worship the Lord as He instructs and honor Him by the shedding of the blood of the lamb. For He said, 'When I see the blood, I will pass over you'" (Exod. 12:13).

The covenant is established in blood, for without the shedding of blood there is no forgiveness of sin (see Heb. 9:22). Thus year after year God instructed His people to spill the blood of the sacrificial lamb to fulfill the requirements of His righteous law and find mercy and favor.

A New Covenant

God foresaw, however, that a new covenant needed to be established. Under this new covenant, God would live within rather than without; because of His indwelling presence, people would be far more sensitive to the things that would destroy them and separate them from God. To establish this new covenant, God needed a blood so pure and powerful that it would be shed as an offering only once to be effective forever— not only to cover sin but to remove its stain totally. No human could be this sacrifice, for the entire human race is tainted with sin. God needed another way. He decided to do it Himself—through the giving of His one and only Son, Jesus the Messiah.

Jesus, the eternal Son, left His throne to love us completely. He died for our sins on the cross and rose from the dead three days later. It is His blood that once applied to any penitent heart not only removes the stain of sin but also brings the gift of eternal life. He has become the Passover Lamb for everyone who puts their trust in Him as their Lord and Savior.

Today to "keep the Passover" can mean to keep the blood of Jesus applied to the doorpost of our hearts. After our initial salvation experience, we need ongoing cleansing, and that is made possible through the continuing and abiding power of the blood of the Lamb! First John 1:9 tells us, "If we confess our sins, He is faithful and just to forgive us our sins and to cleanse us from all unrighteousness."

Just when the caterpillar thought the world was over, it became a butterfly.

Anonymous

Encountering God Today

1. Many of us grew up in an environment that was less than godly, and that influenced our behavior. What does Josiah's life teach us about God's ability to redeem the past and heal us from things the enemy designed to destroy us? What can we learn about God's sovereign grace in our lives that can pick us up where we are and place us where He's called us to be?

2. God was moved by Josiah's tender heart toward Him. The Word of the Lord pierced Josiah, and he responded in brokenness and awe. Why is it important to have a tender heart toward God? Why is it important to remain sensitive to His Word?

3. Josiah cleaned the temple and got rid of the idols. How do we keep a "clean house"? Are there any idols hiding out in the recesses of your "house" that you've forgotten about? Why is it important to keep our lives clean and pure?

4. The story of Josiah shows us what happens when God's Word is not an active part of people's lives. What are ways we can make sure that God's Word has an active part in our walk with the Lord? What positive effects does the reading and memorizing of Scripture have on us?

3

REJOICE IN THE LORD ALWAYS

Finding Strength to Sing Despite Your Circumstances

ACTS 16:16–34; PHILIPPIANS 4:4–7

If you've been a Christian for any length of time, you know that trusting Jesus Christ doesn't exempt you from tests, trials, and trouble. Jesus told us that we would encounter oppression, stress, pressure, anguish, and the like, but He also said to take heart because He has overcome the world—which is the root of such persecution (see John 16:33). Because He has overcome such adversity, through Him we too can overcome. The Holy Spirit dwelling within the believer gives us the power to do so. He is the divine Helper Jesus promised.

Scattered throughout my life are various times in which my family or I have had to walk through some dark days. My mother would often say during such times of test and trial, "Well, we can either laugh or cry . . . I'd rather laugh!" That always made me laugh—literally. But there's more to facing a trial than just laughing, as if you're ignoring the problem or somehow refusing to deal with the situation realistically. Laughter comes from a deep-seated conviction that the Lord will always have the last say—no matter what the doctor's report, no matter how grave the situation looks, no matter how large the enemy seems. God is always in control.

Sometimes I've had to laugh with tears running down my cheeks or with a lump in my throat, but I've gone ahead and laughed anyway because my mom's right. Her advice echoes the apostle Paul, who wrote, "Rejoice in the Lord always. Again I will say, rejoice!" (Phil. 4:4). Paul knew well the importance of rejoicing always. He wrote that line from a prison in Rome! And surely he practiced rejoicing before he told his readers to do it. But how could he rejoice when he was suffering in chains and awaiting his trial? What did he know that we need to know?

It is in sudden testings that our treasure is revealed.

St. Francis of Assisi

A Song Cannot Be Shackled

Ten years before he wrote these now famous words in his letter to the church at Philippi, Paul had been there to introduce the gospel of Jesus Christ to them. While there, he and his friend Silas were beaten and placed in a Philippian jail for casting an evil spirit out of a slave girl. Around midnight, while in shackles, bloodied and with open wounds, and in a dank inner prison, Paul and Silas began to pray and sing to the Lord. How strange it must have seemed there in that terrible place to hear the song of the Lord arise amid the suffering, neglect, and mistreatment. How odd to hear joy coming from such a place of sorrow, and yet how comforting, warm, and inviting their words of praise must have been to those who listened in the dark.

The comfort of their song mirrors the comfort of the Lord that reaches down to any depth to touch a soul in need. The presence of God shows up to those who honor Him, a witness to anyone around that He is real. Paul and Silas could have laughed or cried—they chose to laugh through songs of praise! They knew that Jesus Christ had overcome the world. They knew that "He who is in you is greater than he who is in the world" (1 John 4:4). They learned something that is valuable and vital to our Christian walk: the importance of rejoicing in the Lord, no matter what the circumstance may be.

As they continued to offer up their songs of worship, God responded in a big way, a really big way! While they were singing, an earthquake shook the foundations of the prison so hard that the prison doors burst wide open and even their shackles came off. God's heart was so moved by their worship, their passion for Him, and their determination to rejoice in spite of everything that He showed up in an earthquake.

When the jailer awoke and saw the prison doors opened wide, he thought for sure that everyone had escaped, and he pulled his sword to commit suicide. But from the darkness, Paul called out to him that they were all still there. Is this amazing or what? Rather than escape, they allowed God to use them again to witness to this lost man. The jailer knew the reason for their imprisonment and no doubt had heard about the Lord of whom they testified, for he fell down at the feet of Paul and Silas and asked, "Sirs, what must I do to be saved?" (Acts 16:30).

Before the night was over, the jailer and his entire household received Jesus Christ as their Lord and Savior and were baptized by Paul and Silas. The jailer not only washed their wounds but brought them into his own home and served them a meal.

Our witness can have a profound impact on those who are searching for meaning and purpose. Had Paul and Silas run off at the first sign of those doors opening, they would have missed the opportunity that God had orchestrated. They waited long enough for God to gain the glory. The song of the Lord sustained them and encouraged them until their deliverance came.

There are no crown-wearers in Heaven who were not cross-bearers here below.

Charles Haddon Spurgeon

"Psalming" to the Lord

Before he died, a friend of mine told me something that I will never forget: "You can rule from any prison if you know how to psalm!" His words pierced my heart as I understood clearly what he meant. You can be placed in a physical or even an emotional prison, but the joy of the Lord and your worship offered up to Him can never be imprisoned! You and I can rule from—and in—any situation as long as we rejoice, as long as we psalm, as long as we worship.

My friend's understanding of "psalming" to the Lord came from the apostle Paul. In his letter to the Colossians he wrote, "Let the word of Christ dwell in you richly in all wisdom, teaching and admonishing one another *in psalms and hymns and spiritual songs*, singing with grace in your hearts to the Lord" (Col. 3:16, italics added). He also addressed the church at Ephesus with a similar admonition: "And do not be drunk with wine, in which is dissipation; but be filled with the Spirit, speaking to one another *in psalms and hymns and spiritual songs*, singing and making melody in your heart to the Lord" (Eph. 5:18–19, italics added). Sounds like Paul has a life-theme going here!

Very simply put, *psalms* are Scripture; *hymns* are lyrics of human inspiration set to melody; and *spiritual songs* are spontaneous melodic lyrics given by the Holy Spirit in one's own tongue or spiritual language. Our regular participation in singing psalms, hymns, and spiritual songs can help us memorize God's Word and aid us in sustaining a Spirit-filled life. Every follower of Jesus Christ gains strength by recalling the

Lord's promises in His Word through song. By putting Scripture to your own music or making up your own melody as you sing the Word, you soon discover that it has a profound impact on you no matter the circumstance. You can rule from any prison if you know how to psalm.

Dwell in possibility.
Emily Dickinson

Worship That Rules

What we are talking about is worship—worship that rules, worship that rules over every adverse situation and circumstance! Worship that rules is worship where the lordship of Jesus Christ is bestowed and sustained because of our praise and rejoicing. He has promised in Psalm 22:3 to show up and inhabit our praise at any time and at any place where it is offered. He inhabits the praises of His people, whether it's in a prison cell in Philippi or a field in Kansas. God's heart is warmed and moved when His children love Him through their praises and adoration. He shows up—sometimes in big ways—when we call on Him.

Our rejoicing in worship is not just a mood or mere emotion. Within our worship of the Holy there lies an understanding of who we are as His children. We understand, aided by the Scriptures and the Holy Spirit, that whether the day brings great joy or deep sorrow, the Lord stands in the midst of it all with us—active on our behalf because of His great love for us. God is still in control. As believers, we soon realize that our song cannot be silenced by pain, suffering, circumstance, weakness, or trial. Our song emanates from our heart—a heart that has received Him and claimed Him as Lord and Savior. Our praise becomes His address as we enthrone Him with our worship.

There is no doubt that the Psalms both taught and brought great comfort to Paul and Silas. David, like Paul, was no stranger to adversity. One of David's most beloved psalms was written from a cave—a prison— where he was hiding out from the wrath of King Saul. Here in the midst of this cave, running for his life, David begins to rejoice in the Lord. He writes:

> David knew that God transcends our circumstances for He is *still* in control no matter how things look to us.

My heart is steadfast, O God, my heart is
    steadfast;
I will sing and give praise.
Awake, my glory!
Awake, lute and harp!
I will awaken the dawn.
I will praise You, O Lord, among the peoples;
I will sing to You among the nations.
For Your mercy reaches unto the heavens,
And Your truth unto the clouds.
Be exalted, O God, above the heavens;
Let Your glory be above all the earth.

                                    Psalm 57:7–11

Sounds to me like rejoicing in the Lord always.

David was in a "prison," facing death, running for his life, nowhere else to go, and through the power of worship, he began to rule from inside the cave. In the early part of Psalm 57 he mentions the evil forces arrayed against him and how the enemy has sought to destroy him, and yet David knew that God transcends our circumstances for He is *still* in control no matter how things look to us. Of course God did deliver David many times during the course of his life. David's example shows us clearly that even "anointed people" praise God anyway!

Joy is a defiant *nevertheless*!

Karl Barth

Always Rejoice in the Lord

Have you ever been in a prison? Maybe it hasn't been a physical place of incarceration, but have you ever been in a prison of your own? From time to time we may find ourselves in prison—a prison of sickness, accusation, financial ruin, loss and heartache, circumstances beyond our control, an emotional prison because of things that happened to us long ago. Most anything can become a prison.

The important thing is not the *kind* of prison you find yourself in but *what you are going to do when you are in that prison.* What are you going to do when you're running for your life, suddenly in a situation that is beyond your control? I encourage you to *rejoice!* Praise God! Psalm unto the Lord! Sing the Scripture!

Sing God's Word! Sing His promises! God is bigger than whatever is facing you right now. Circumstances will always change, but God will never change.

Whether Paul was singing in chains or writing letters of encouragement to the church from his prison cell—from one prison to another, from one experience to another—he kept singing, he kept praising, and he kept rejoicing! He knew that circumstantial confinement had nothing to do with his ability to worship the Lord. The joy of the Lord is our strength (Neh. 8:10), and our weakest moments are when that strength can show itself in a mighty way (2 Cor. 12:9), because every part of our being is totally surrendered and relying on Him. It is when we come to the end of ourselves, clearly recognizing that we cannot accomplish a thing apart from God, that we find the song within welling up, finding expression on our lips.

Sometimes with tears streaming down our cheeks, sometimes lying awake in the dark, sometimes when words fail us, there arises within a song. Aided by the precious Holy Spirit, the urge to praise and rejoice surfaces during the most unlikely circumstances. We've all seen it, in our own lives or in the lives of those we know—that deep-seated joy that steels a heart in the midst of a battle, that brings calm in the midst of a storm, that pours out the oil and wine in the midst of a wasteland. It is the joy of the Lord—our strength.

When you exercise worship that rules, it puts God between you and your circumstance, between you and your calamity, between you and the source of your bondage. Worship and rejoicing will help you rule over your emotions, your circumstances, your enemies, your adversities—whatever seeks to imprison you. Your praise will always establish a base of operation for God's wonder-working power. If you will rejoice, He will work it out. He always has and He always will. Worship is a defiant _"nevertheless"_ in the face of circumstances beyond our control.

Read the stories of people in the Bible who worshiped in the midst of their adversity and experienced God's deliverance:

- Isaac—Genesis 26:1–13
- Joseph—Genesis 37–45
- Moses—Exodus 3–15
- Elijah—1 Kings 17
- David—Psalm 54, 57; 1 Samuel 23–24
- Job—Job 1
- Jonah—Jonah 2
- Habakkuk—Habakkuk 3:17–18
- Words of Jesus—Matthew 5:1–16

Encountering God Today

1. Though Paul and Silas were treated unfairly and were put in prison unjustly, their response was not one of protest but rather of trusting God for their deliverance and vindication. What can we learn from their faith in God that will help us when we are treated unfairly or falsely accused?

2. Paul clearly teaches by example that although you can be bound in body, your spirit and soul can still be free. Rather than being brought down by his circumstances, Paul overcame them by continuously praying and worshiping the Lord. Think of a recent unexpected and difficult circumstance in your life. What was your response? Did you rejoice in the Lord?

3. It is in communion with God that we more fully realize His redemptive gifts and His nearness, which cannot be destroyed by pain, suffering, weakness, or difficult circumstances. When you worship God during a difficult time, what effect does it have on your outlook and your faith?

4. Psalm 57 was written during a difficult time in David's life. What does his situation teach you about godly people encountering tests and trials? Why is it important to remember that like David, we should worship and praise God, even if we find ourselves running for our lives?

4

BUILD ALTARS OF UNCUT STONE

The Art of Becoming a Living Sacrifice

EXODUS 20:22–26; DEUTERONOMY 27:1–6

I grew up in the church. Both of my parents were ministers, and my brother and I found ourselves with a lot of time on our hands while Mom and Dad were busy counseling, having meetings, or working in their offices. What was really fun for us were the times prior to and after each service, when we, along with the other staff kids, would think of adventurous things to do or, better yet, dare someone else to do. Our sanctuary had a wooden altar rail that stretched almost the entire width of the room. We soon found out that the altar was big enough and sturdy enough for a kid to stand on or even swing on. For whatever reason, we would dare each other to do such "sacrilegious" things, and inevitably an usher or the janitor would come running toward us saying, "You kids get off that altar!"

Years later as a college student, I laughed about such things, and the thought occurred to me that the janitor was wrong! Though my motives as a child were different, my actions then are what God wants from me now. He wants me on the altar. Satan certainly doesn't want me there, but my love for and service to God demand it.

Uncut Stones

After receiving the Ten Commandments, God instructed Moses on the type of altar His people were to build for offering sacrifices of worship. God said, "And there you shall build an altar to the LORD your God, an altar of stones; you shall not use any iron tool on them. You shall build with whole [uncut] stones the altar of the LORD your God, and offer burnt offerings on it to the LORD your God" (Deut. 27:5–6). God wanted them to build an altar with rough, uncut stones. He didn't want ornate, decorated, religious-looking, beautiful, gemlike stones. He wanted whatever they could find— that would be good enough! Uncut stones—rocks, fieldstones, boulders—look so imperfect to the human eye, and yet not one of us could create even a little pebble. Each stone is unique.

When looking into the mirror of our lives, we can see the past (whether we like it or not). We can see where we've failed, where we've made mistakes, and where our weaknesses are. After examining our life, we often come to the conclusion that we are disqualified from meaningful ministry because we're not perfect. We all are frail beings who fail often, and sometimes we leave various opportunities to serve, which God brings *our* way, to others (who we think are more qualified and less human than we are).

You see, we have heard the call of God's Word to "present your bodies a living sacrifice, holy, acceptable to God, which is your reasonable service" (Rom. 12:1), and immediately, on hearing that call, we begin to focus on the building of the altar on which we intend to sacrifice ourselves to the Lord and His work. Even though our altars are made up of our imperfect past and present, our good days and bad, we do our best to build beautiful altars that are attractive. Finding ordinary stones, we want to spend an inordinate amount of time fashioning them into beautiful, symmetrically cut stones. We want to arrange them in such a way that they inspire us to ooh and aah. We try to make the stones that are found in the field of our lives look good and fit together closely. But there's a problem.

After scanning the ground and moving the stones about, we realize that the stones of life are uneven—some big, some little, some round and smooth, others large and jagged. They don't seem to fit very well together, and they certainly don't look holy. We get discouraged, anxious, and even disappointed because we don't have the perfect stones that will line up well. So we go to work trying to smooth the rough edges and cutting them to look religious so that we can build a proper altar to God.

We get caught up in the building of our altar: what it's supposed to look like, what kind of building materials we will need, and in what style we will build it. While we do this, we miss the command of the Lord that sets us free from all worry and wasted time: God wants altars of uncut stones. God wants altars that are untouched by human efforts for perfection. Don't waste your energy on the altar material—invest in the sacrifice that will go on top of the altar. You and I are the sacrifices—living sacrifices to God's glory!

> Commonly there are three stages in work for God: impossible, difficult, done!
>
> Hudson Taylor

Altars Are for Sacrifices

Several years ago I stood in the great York Minster in England, admiring the high altar and its accoutrements. As I took it all in, the gentle voice of the Holy Spirit spoke to my heart and said, "This is all wrong, all wrong. Altars are not places of beauty to be admired; they are to be places of sacrifice, places of death." Immediately I understood what the Lord was communicating to me that day: an altar is a place where I die to my will, my way, and my desires, and surrender to the will of the One who loved me first and loves me best. An altar should be covered in tears of worship, tears of struggle, tears of frustration, and tears of joy.

God does not accept the altar; He accepts the sacrifice that's placed on the altar. We don't read in God's Word, "And God consumed the altar." No! We read, "And God consumed the sacrifice"(Lev. 9:24; Judg. 6:21; 2 Chron. 7:1). You see, altars are not holy because of who built them or what they're made of. An altar is holy because of what is on it. Today, as in Old Testament times, altars are built in response to an encounter with the living God.

Altars are memorials not to the dead but to the living Lord who transcends the daily lives of ordinary, everyday people like you and me. Ordinary and everyday lives—like rough-edged and odd-sized stones—always make the best altars on which to offer our hearts to God. This truth helps to dismantle the lies of the enemy: "You're not good enough"; "You're not ready yet"; "Your altar could never be as beautiful as their altar." When we believe such lies, we are led to doing nothing at all, a kind of spiritual inertia, and many times we want to give up.

Feelings of unworthiness and condemnation are not from God. He has called us to build our altars out of uncut, ordinary stones found in the fields of our lives.

> God does not accept the altar; He accepts the sacrifice that's placed on the altar.

God does not build altars; we do. But in the building of altars, we must not lose sight of the fact that it is the sacrifice—not the appearance of the altar—that matters to the Lord. What is significant to God is the fact that we love Him so much that we are willing to sacrifice our agenda for His, our plans for His, our way for His, our character for His, and our attitudes for His.

Use the Altar Daily

Under the old covenant, the altar was the center of daily activity for God's people. All hours of the day and night, the priests kept the fire burning on God's altar, always ready for when the people needed to offer a sacrifice. The perpetual fire let the people know that the way to God was always open. The priests were always there to offer the sacrifices of the faithful. Thus God provided a way for sin to be dealt with and for people to live with a clear conscience. When the people made sacrifices, God was willing to extend forgiveness, mercy, and grace. Of course this all foreshadowed what was to come in the ministry and sacrifice of Jesus.

My parents used to teach us to keep a "short sin account." In other words, never allow sin and disobedience to pile up in your heart and go unchecked and unforgiven. The minute the "still small voice" of the Holy Spirit convicts you of something you did or said, ask the Lord to forgive you. Don't wait; do it right away. Thank God that He has provided a new and Living Way for us of forgiveness, mercy, and grace, a way that allows us to come before Him, submitting ourselves to Him and receiving forgiveness for our confessed sins. Jesus Christ, God's one and only Son, is that way for all people, allowing access to ongoing cleansing and healing. He's always ready to forgive.

Don't allow the altar in your life to go unused or neglected. We shouldn't waste precious time trying to act religious when what we all need is a relationship that calls us to a place of daily devotion. We must become living sacrifices surrendered to God on the altar of life. Even as the Old Testament sacrifices created a pleasing aroma to the Lord, our lives lived to bring glory to Him are pleasing as well. Second Corinthians 2:14–15 tells us: "Now thanks be to God who always leads us in triumph in Christ, and through us diffuses the fragrance of His knowledge in every place. For we are to God the fragrance of Christ among those who are being saved and among those who are perishing."

Consider that even in the tabernacle and temple worship of God's people in the Old Testament, the altar was also a place where incense was burned perpetually before the Lord. Only the fire from the altar could be used to burn the incense (Lev. 16:12; Num. 16:46). Thus the same holy fire that consumed the sacrifice also consumed the incense. This incense both foreshadowed and symbolized the prayers and worship of God's people (Ps. 141:2; Rev. 5:8). When we come to God at the altar of sacrifice to offer prayer and praise, it is an aroma that is so pleasing to Him. There at the altars of our lives, Jesus's cleansing blood mingles with the fragrance of our penitent words and the distinctive scent of our worship.

Collectively as Christians, our lives become the uncut stones that God uses to build His church—the body of Christ—where spiritual sacrifices are offered daily in loving worship. The apostle Peter reminded the church, "You also, as living stones, are being built up a spiritual house, a holy priesthood, to offer up spiritual sacrifices acceptable to God through Jesus Christ" (1 Peter 2:5). Under the new covenant, you and I are now the priests offering up the sacrifices of our very selves, surrendered and yielded to His heart.

> Faith goes up the stairs that love has made and looks out the window which hope has opened.
>
> Charles Haddon Spurgeon

The Cross—an Altar

Far from the beautiful crosses that adorn churches, cathedrals, and abbeys across this world, the cross Jesus used to offer Himself was made of everyday rough wood—an altar made of wood on which the Prince of Peace would sacrifice His life. It was not beautiful, nothing special to look at, but its beauty was found in what was offered on it—the Sacrifice—the Lamb of God. And His sacrifice was pleasing to God, our Father, for He consumed the Sacrifice completely so that sin, death, hell, and the grave could be dealt with once and for all for all humankind. Everlasting life was purchased for us through Jesus's sacrifice. As imitators of Christ and doers of His Word, we should follow His example and lay down our lives for His purposes and plans.

We must stop wasting our time using man-made tools to construct altars that look religious and dignified. God loves the beauty of the stones in our lives. Think about it: even when the Lord sent Nehemiah to rebuild the broken-down walls of Jerusalem, He did not require that Nehemiah use new stones. Instead, God told Nehemiah to use the old burned and damaged stones that had fallen down into the valley floor. He told him to pick them up and reuse them. The importance wasn't placed on what the stones looked like; the importance was placed on their use and on Nehemiah's obedience to God's Word.

Whoever you are and wherever in life you may be, God calls you to take the rubble of your past and use it to build a holy altar to Him. Don't allow any unused altars to be built in your life. Remember what the Lord told Moses? He warned him that if an iron tool was used to cut the stones, He would consider them profane. God made it clear to Moses (and to us) that we are not to waste our efforts on what material the altar is made from—rather, we should invest in the sacrifice that goes on the altar. The next time someone tells you to "get off that altar," don't you dare!

Take my hands and let them move at the impulse of Thy love.

Frances Ridley Havergal

Encountering God Today

1. What image does the word *altar* bring to your mind? Is it related to what a real altar was used for? Why is the "altar" still a powerful symbol in the church?

2. When God gives instructions, He intends them to be followed. Why do you think the Lord was so specific about the type of stones to be used in building an altar to Him? What are our lives saying to the Lord when we are obedient to the instruction in His Word?

3. If we're honest with ourselves, we admit to doing things to try to impress other people. Can you think of a time or place in your life when you spent more time working on how something looked on the outside than on the inside? What was the outcome?

4. Human achievement can get us only so far in life. We need the presence of the Lord in our hearts and lives to lead, guide, and direct us. Romans 12:1 calls us to present ourselves in worship at God's altar as *living sacrifices*. How and when do we accomplish that?

5

REACH FOR JESUS

Allowing Christ's Touch
to Change Your Life

MATTHEW 9:18–22; MARK 5:21–34

If one considered life as a simple loan, one would
perhaps be less exacting. We possess actually nothing;
everything goes through us.

Eugene Delacroix

In fourth grade my friends and I had a lot of fun se-
cretly placing "Kick Me" signs on other kids' backs.
Half the fun was found in the daring challenge of getting the sign in place without the poor soul's knowing

it. The longer the sign remained in place the funnier it was. It usually took a while for the recipient to figure out why everyone kept trying to kick the back of their legs and feet. Of course when they were kicked, they weren't as amused as we were. Though we meant no harm, it was still embarrassing for the one we chose to be a walking advertisement for adversity.

Imagine going through life with a "Kick Me" sign on your back! There are a lot of folks who don't have to imagine—for them it is a reality. The "sign" was not placed there by a group of kids just having some fun either. It's as if life placed it there. Something that happened to them, a difficult situation, or an unfortunate event has left them scarred, sick, hurt, and traumatized, and it shows. Our society is full of such people—people with physical deformities, AIDS, or a speech impediment; people who are homeless; people with emotional problems, all kinds of infirmities for which there seem to be no cure; even people whose skin is a different color from that of the majority. The list goes on and on. These people suffer from the silent stares of others who either don't know what to say or find it too uncomfortable to be around them.

But there is hope for people who suffer like this. The Word of God is full of societal outcasts who had inspiring stories. They became people whom God chose to use and bless with His favor. They were healed inside and out by the hand of God. Such people reveal to us over and over again that God is no respecter of persons, and what He's done for someone else, He'll do for you as well. The Lord loves us all and has demonstrated His divine love through Jesus Christ, the Son of God. Jesus is not only "the Word made flesh," but He is also love incarnate. He has a way of reaching through our layers, defenses, walls, excuses, and even "Kick Me" signs to see us all for who we really are.

Feeling Desperate

Both Mark and Matthew record a story of a societal outcast. For twelve long years, this particular woman had sought a cure for her physical infirmity—an infirmity that had left her with constant bleeding. Perhaps worse than the drain on her physical strength and finances was the stigma of uncleanness. In Jewish society, if a woman experienced bleeding she was considered unclean until the bleeding stopped (Lev. 15:19–27). She was to be around no one and touch no one for any reason. Furthermore, it was her responsibility as someone "unclean" to stay away from everything and everyone.

The woman had spent twelve years with this infirmity. The Bible doesn't tell us how she made it financially. Maybe she was living off her deceased husband's savings or an inheritance from a family member—whatever the case, there was no money left. She had gone through all of her savings seeking a cure. Every resource had been used in the hope of finding healing. Because she was considered defiled, anything and anyone she touched became defiled as well. She couldn't worship in the temple. Thus her sickness had cut her off physically, socially, and spiritually. Trying to find a cure, doctors experimented on her, but after twelve years of working on her, nothing had changed. She had reached the end of her resources. There was, it seemed, no other prospect.

In our search for a "cure," we run from place to place seeking answers, seeking fulfillment, and seeking healing. And after talking to everybody about our condition, after getting everyone's input and opinion, after trying every old remedy in the book, we find ourselves right where we started, because the answer to what ails us is beyond ourselves. It is beyond the natural realm. It lies in the hands of the Healer of every sickness, every broken heart, and every broken life. Whether our sickness is physical or spiritual, Jesus Christ is still the Christ of every crisis. He is the answer. He is our healing inside and out.

There's one thing about people who have reached the end of their rope—they'll try anything. Desperate people will try anything, and this woman was desperate. Finally she had reached a place where she was willing to break all the social rules, to be misunderstood, to be made fun of and scoffed at, to crawl if she had to, because she was desperate and she had heard that this Jesus of Nazareth was headed her way and He had the power to heal. In her desperation, she would do a daring thing—she would reach out and touch Jesus.

The Bible says that she walked behind Jesus in the crowd. That was the appropriate place for defiled people to walk—at the back of the crowd. Defiled people always came last. You can sense her twelve years of frustration, twelve years of tears in the night, twelve years of having doctors poke and prod, twelve years of pain and turmoil, and here she was just an arm's length from healing. *If I can touch—just touch Him—there'll be no more bleeding, no more discomfort, no more being an outcast, no more doctors' experiments, no more sickness.*

She believed in Jesus all right—that's why she was in the crowd. She heard over and over what He had done for others. She heard that He was no respecter of persons and that He loved everyone. This was it! Nothing was going to stop her now. If she could get close enough just to touch even the edge of His clothing—just His clothing—she knew that would be enough to heal her. *If He's that awesome, that powerful, if He is the Son of God, surely one touch of His clothing will be enough.* She did not have to hold on—just a touch! As desperation set in, the answer to her prayers was on its way.

The power of God was already beginning to flood her heart as she reached out to touch the Son of God. And then it happened, quick as a blink of an eye! She touched His garment for only a moment, but that's all it took. Suddenly she knew; she felt it from head to toe; she could sense His healing power rippling through her body. Something had changed. Something was different. She hadn't felt this good in twelve years. She was healed! Not a word had been spoken. She simply reached out and touched Him. Her need was met by His goodness and love.

God graciously uses our simple needs to train us and prepare us for something much higher than we were thinking of. We were seeking gifts: He, the Giver, longs to give us Himself!

Andrew Murray

Who Touched Me?

As she stopped to take it all in, suddenly she heard Jesus say, "Who touched me?" The disciples must have thought, *He must be joking*! There were hoards of people pressing against Him as they moved shoulder to shoulder through the street. But Jesus insisted that someone had touched Him, not just bumped into Him, not just brushed up against Him. He knew someone had touched Him on purpose. Jesus knew this because He felt power go out of Him at the moment of her touch. The Lord's perception of what had happened corresponded to the woman's expectation that healing would take place through contact with the Healer.

Jesus asked more directly, "Who touched My clothes?" Think of this: out of all the people who were bumping into Jesus, brushing up against Him, pressing into Him, only one touched Him on purpose. Only one reached out to Him in faith. Only one touched Him with the expectation that the impossible would become possible. Why would Jesus stop and ask who touched Him when surely He knew who it was? Most likely He wanted to help that precious woman make an open confession—so important to salvation (Rom. 10:10)—but also to make it clear that the object of her faith was Himself and not His clothing.

Mark 5:33 says, "But the woman, fearing and trembling, knowing what had happened to her, came and fell down before Him and told Him the whole truth." I don't think her reaction was due to guilt from breaking the law, that is, a defiled person touching Jesus, but rather one of awe and adoration at what she was now feeling within her own body. Her reaction was simply one of heartfelt gratitude and worship as she fell at the feet of Jesus.

The Lord responded to her by calling her affectionately, "Daughter . . ." He was not angry; He was not upset; He was in fact overwhelmed by this woman's faith in Him, a faith that would reach through the crowd, through the press of people. Jesus pronounced her healed, affirmed her faith, and told her to walk and live in peace.

Never Too Busy

The story of the outcast woman actually takes place within the context of a larger story about a man's request for Jesus to heal his sick and dying twelve-year-old daughter. The beauty of this whole narrative is this: Jesus was never too busy to meet someone's need. As Jesus was on His way to Jairus's house, the hemorrhaging woman made her move. Her faith reached out and touched Jesus while He was just passing through. But Jesus allowed Himself to be stopped, His journey interrupted. He allowed His agenda to wait and altered His travel plans just a bit to heal the woman's infirmity. Praise the Lord! After He had healed her, He went on and raised Jairus's daughter from the dead. Jesus has the power over disease and death. He is Lord of all.

Jesus is *never* too busy to meet your needs.

Jesus is *never* too busy to meet your needs. You can interrupt Him anytime and anyplace. He is more than happy to heal you today. He is more than thrilled to meet your need right now. He's always on His way somewhere, but since He's passing through, why don't you seize the moment? Why don't you let your faith arise and reach out to receive your miracle today?

Every once in a while, the strains of an old hymn come back to me and remind me of this subject. One of my fondest childhood memories is our church singing this song. It instilled in me a truth: Jesus is never too busy to meet my need for Him. Both then and now I find comfort in its words:

> Pass me not, O gentle Savior;
> Hear my humble cry.
> While on others Thou art calling,
> Do not pass me by.
> Savior, Savior,
> Hear my humble cry.
> While on others Thou art calling,
> Do not pass me by.
>
> Fannie J. Crosby

Let Your Faith Reach Out

Like the woman who was healed, you and I need to allow our faith to reach beyond our circumstances today. Allow your faith in what God can do move you through any barriers you perceive, just as the woman moved through the crowd. She didn't let the crowd hinder her. Don't let anything stand in your way of reaching out and touching Jesus Christ today. This woman couldn't have cared less how many people were standing around Jesus. All she knew, all she was thinking about, all she dreamed about the night before was *I must touch Him! I must touch Him! I must touch Jesus!* Human effort cannot heal you, but a holy boldness can access healing. This is a boldness that wells up in your heart saying, "Jesus, I want everything You've provided for me. I receive it now." Nothing can stop that kind of determination.

The woman was sick of her sickness. She had had it and could wait no longer. She was out of money, out of doctors, out of time, and probably going out of her mind. But when you're desperate, you're willing to try anything. Desperate people are all-or-nothing people. They want something that will set them free.

How many people today (including you and me) run in and out of church, in and out of His Presence, in and out of worship, bump into Jesus here, run into Jesus there, never expecting, never believing, never taking advantage of the opportunity to receive what we need? When we're desperate enough, when we've reached the end of our resources, when we've come to the end of ourselves, we'll crawl if we have to, pushing our way through a crowd because we know He's the Answer to our need. He's the Healer of our situation. He's the Provider for our lack. He's the Son of the living God.

We can reach for Jesus in a multitude of ways. Through the years I have noticed that His touch has come to me many times through the lives of others. Remember when Jesus said:

> "For I was hungry and you gave Me food; I was thirsty and you gave Me drink; I was a stranger and you took Me in; I was naked and you clothed Me; I was sick and you visited Me; I was in prison and you came to Me."
>
> Then the righteous will answer Him, saying, "Lord, when did we see You hungry and feed You, or thirsty and give You drink? When did we see You a stranger and take You in, or naked and clothe You? Or when did we see You sick, or in prison, and come to You?" And the King will answer and say to them, "Assuredly, I say to you, inasmuch as you did it to one of the least of these My brethren, you did it to Me."
>
> Matthew 25:35–40

Almost without fail, every time I've had the privilege of ministering to others, the Lord ends up ministering back to me through their words, their smiles, their eyes, their touch—because we are in fact touching Him when we reach out to touch others in His name.

We can also reach out to the Lord through writing down a prayer or a poem or song. People who are artistic may pour out their prayer in drawings or paintings. Sometimes it's as simple as memorizing a passage of Scripture or listening to Christian music.

Jesus's response to our touch will come in various ways and forms. As I mentioned above, sometimes it comes through the people to whom we minister. I've also received His touch through the artwork of others: stained glass that filters shafts of sunlight reminding me that He has indeed come to color our world with beauty, paintings of the Lord's life that have left me speechless, sculptures representing the passion of Jesus. They have all left me with a sense of His touch and a greater understanding of His mercy and love.

Of course, the glory of God's creation holds within its power the ability to move our hearts toward Him. Who could ever deny the overwhelming sense of awe we feel when standing on the edge of the Grand Canyon or beside the roar of the Pacific Ocean, or even sitting on the patio in our yard listening to the birds. The same God who made all of this loves us more than we can ever imagine!

There are so many ways to reach out to Christ, and so many ways that He can meet your needs. Why don't you press in today and touch Him on purpose? Don't be satisfied to be in the crowd as an onlooker or a casual observer. No! He's passing by. Get into position. He's headed your way. Let faith arise. Don't allow the stigma of religion to keep you from a relationship with the Living Lord. The answer is drawing near. Reach out and touch Him. Find a way to feel His nearness. Ask Him in prayer to reveal Himself to you. Read His

Word to get to know Him as your true Friend. Just one touch will change your life for all eternity.

> I pray that what is scattered in me may be brought together, so that no part of me may be apart from You.

St. Augustine

Encountering God Today

1. Have you ever felt as if a "Kick Me" sign was attached to your back? If so, when and why?

2. We all face hardships from time to time. Though we'd like to avoid them, they are inevitable. How can God's presence in the midst of a hardship or tough time make a difference? Can you remember such a time?

3. The woman with the infirmity had spent twelve years seeking a cure only to exhaust herself and her resources. What is the significance of coming to the end of ourselves and realizing that only Jesus Christ is the answer to what ails us? Have you ever sought a "cure" somewhere else prior to taking the matter to the Lord?

4. Desperate people do desperate things. Can you think of a time when you had to "press through the crowd" to get what you needed? Is anyone you know communicating signs of desperation? Think of ways to let the person know that Jesus is near and He has the answer.

Excellent

6

BUILD MEMORIALS

Creating a Place of Remembrance

JOSHUA 3:1–4:24

On the campus of the university I attended sits a prayer chapel built of wood with modern stained-glass windows that overlook the Pacific Ocean. Barely big enough for ten people, the chapel was built to be an intimate spot where students can get away to be alone with God.

That little chapel, with its breathtaking views and salty ocean smell, was a place of peace for me time and again. Today, when I get the opportunity to visit or drive by the chapel, I smile and think of all the things God spoke to my heart in that place of solitude and prayer.

Do you remember such a place, a place where you stood or sat or knelt and felt the presence of God, a place where God showed up, a place where He spoke something to your heart, a place where your strength was renewed?

Over the years I have returned to specific places where God spoke to me, called me to the ministry, gave me direction, and gathered me when my insides were scattered. Most of us can recall locations like this—devotional places where we felt the presence of God. When we can, we need to return to these places to remember that God was good to us, God was faithful to us, and God heard our prayers. We must not forget God's intervention in our life.

When I return to these places of His grace, I am reminded of His work in my life. To go back gives me perspective on where I came from. These places help me see how far I've come and how much I've grown. At times they also reveal to me how far I've strayed and thus serve to convict me of sin.

Remembering where we've been can propel us into dreaming of where we might go and into realizing that only God can get us there.

We do not remember days, we remember moments.

Cesare Pavese

A Duty to Remember

When Joshua assumed leadership of several million people in the newborn nation of Israel, he faced heavy obstacles. Following in the footsteps of Moses was intimidating enough. Moses had seen God, personally received the Ten Commandments, and had the people's respect. Joshua was fit for the task of leading, but he had yet to face his first major challenge. Then Israel approached the shores of the swollen Jordan River. The flood-stage river lay between Israel's past of brutal Egyptian slavery and her future of an abundant life in the Promised Land.

The Lord had given Joshua instructions for crossing the Jordan River. Following these instructions, the priests carried the ark of the covenant—the representation of God's presence—to the riverbank. As soon as their feet felt the cool water, the water from upstream came to an abrupt halt. Miraculously, the water piled up in a heap a great distance away. The riverbed, which minutes before held flood-level waters, was now as dry as the desert the Israelites had just crossed.

This first miracle under Joshua's ministry proved that God was with him as He had been with Moses, establishing Joshua as the divinely called leader of Israel. It inspired God's people and scared their enemies to death. Up until this time, the river had served as protection for the peoples of Canaan. Now the Amorites and the Canaanites knew that the Lord God of Israel could not be stopped. His will and purposes were to be fulfilled for His chosen people—river or no river!

The priests stood in the middle of the river with the ark of the covenant. All around them, God's people walked through the dust, reliving their parents' stories about the Red Sea's parting. When the entire nation of Israel had reached the other side of the Jordan, God told Joshua to choose twelve men, one from each tribe, and instructed each to place twelve stones from the Jordan riverbed where they were to stay that night. And so the Israelites erected a memorial to the Lord. God instructed them to build Him a memorial first *during* their deliverance, and then, later, He commanded them to take those same stones and build a memorial to Him again, *after* their victorious deliverance from their enemies (see Josh. 4:9, 20).

The passage gives three distinct reasons for building the stone memorial:

1. The current generation entering the land will need a memorial, because the days ahead will be challenging at best.

2. The generations to come will need a memorial so they remember the faith of their parents and ancestors.

3. The memorial will testify to others that God is real and cares for His people.

The last verse of chapter 4 strikes this note: "He did this so that all the peoples of the earth might know that the hand of the LORD is powerful and so that you might always fear the LORD your God" (NIV). Francis Schaeffer says, "The stones were to tell the other nations roundabout that this God is different. He really exists; he is a living God, a God of real power who is immanent in the world" (*Joshua and the Flow of Biblical History* [Downers Grove, IL: InterVarsity, 1975], 87).

Just like the children of Israel, we need memorials. Without memory triggers, we tend to forget the goodness and power of the Lord God on our behalf. Those uncut stones set up by Joshua in Gilgal stood as a testimony of the past and a witness to the future: a shrine to the duty of remembering—and the danger of forgetting—the Lord God. In an age when books were rare and monuments were relied on to stir remembrance, those stones proclaimed to succeeding generations the guidance and government of God. You and I need to establish memorials in our spiritual journey. By doing so we

- keep a record of our experiences with God,
- have something to share with others to instruct them in how to be faithful,
- are reminded of God's faithfulness in the past, which will encourage our faith in the present.

Remembrance Stones

We each have our own "remembrance stones," those places in our lives where we especially felt God's presence. The church has remembrance stones too. The Lord's Supper is a constant reminder of Jesus's unfathomable love for you and me and all who are lost in sin. The day that you were saved is a memorial in your past, as is your baptism.

There are many times in our lives when we must recognize memorials to the Lord. Times we need to remember could include healings, special blessings from God, the sparing of a life during a disaster or accident, an answer to prayer, a marriage covenant, a timely job, winning someone to the Lord, the provision of a home, a situation God delivered us from, the lives of our children—any point of divine intervention.

When looking back over a life of faithfulness to the Lord and His Word, we should see miles upon miles of memorials to God's faithfulness, hundreds or thousands of instances when God's love and mercy intervened, places that are marked by a specific time and date—a moment in time that affected everything that followed. It is our duty as believers in Jesus Christ to remember the times He delivered us and brought us across to the other side on dry ground.

A Place Where We Return

Many people return to the place where they were born, the school they attended as a child, or a church they grew up in to "get in touch with their roots." Have you ever gone back to visit a place from your childhood and been surprised to see how much it had shrunk? When I was a kid, I thought a person could get lost in our cavernous three-story home, not to mention the school's playground that seemed to go on forever. Now I see that it was an average size home and that the little fenced playground is just big enough for a game of kick ball. Perspective is everything!

Yet I wouldn't trade anything for a single moment in those places. How many lessons did I learn from my parents in that house—lessons of faith in God, trusting in God, and the love of God? How many times did my parents pray for me before I left the house to walk to school, to remind me that God is with me wherever I go and will never leave me?

As we have opportunity, we need to return to the places of our past—especially those significant to our faith—to remember God's goodness, faithfulness, and the history of His answering our prayers. When I return to these places, such as my childhood home or that tiny prayer chapel, I remember His great power and loving guidance in my life.

> For now we are pilgrims . . . walking by the kind of faith that holds fast to the inner vision of what we shall be when He appears.
>
> St. Augustine

A Place Where Our Children Return

I remember vividly a childhood trip with my father to visit *his* childhood home along the banks of the Ohio River. In the days before dams, springtime meant flooding to those who lived along the river, and my father's childhood house had succumbed to the waters many times. My grandparents were poor, so moving wasn't an option. Thus the almost annual ritual of cleaning the mud out of the house and restoring the floor and walls became an exercise in faith as they trusted God to see them through. And He did, time after time.

My mother grew up poor as well. She has shown me several places where she lived with her five brothers and sisters. When I see their humble beginnings, I can't help but be grateful. God has protected and watched over each of them throughout their lives. He has blessed them abundantly.

My parents traveled in ministry across the country for many years, often sharing with me their firsthand "praise reports" of how God moved in miraculous ways. They tell of God's intervention with financial support, physical healing, and opened doors of opportunity. I share these personal examples with you to demonstrate how the older generations can teach children about the goodness of God.

Joel 1:3 says, "Tell it to your children, and let your children tell it to their children, and their children to the next generation" (NIV). It is important to verbally express what God has done in your life and how He has intervened on your behalf. The next generation needs to know what God has done. They need to hear of His faithfulness, mercy, love, protection, and blessings. Young people's attitudes toward God and their receptivity to Him depend on mature Christians sharing about their own walk with the Lord. Let them know your history with God—how He has been there for you time and time again. Telling others about God's greatness and His provision will open their hearts to believe that God can and will do the same for them and their children.

As parents, my wife and I pray with our children every day before they go to school. We want them to know that everything in their lives matters to the Lord and that they will never have to face any situation alone. The very act of praying with your children will leave in their lives a place of remembrance.

Leave easily recognizable landmarks of faith for your children so that they can say to their children, "Let me tell you about the day that Grandma laid her hands on a sick person and he was healed," or "Let me tell you about the time that Grandpa didn't have a job and God brought them through with a miracle in their finances." That is a true legacy!

A Place for Others to See

I remember my first visit to Notre Dame de Paris. The cathedral began as one man's vision and turned into a reality that has ministered to untold millions of people. Maurice de Sully, bishop of Paris, wanted to build a church that would be the center of Christianity for the people of Paris and indeed all of France. Because it took eighty-seven years to build (AD 1163–1250), de Sully died fifty-four years before its completion. Yet he lived long enough to see that his vision to build a place of worship for God's people would be realized.

As I sat in the midst of that vast holy place, I wondered about the millions upon millions of prayers that had been lifted to heaven there, the songs of praise that had been offered, and the lives of those who had received from God's open hands of blessing. I was glad that Maurice de Sully had built that church; I'm sure heaven is as well.

Whether it is Notre Dame de Paris or a clapboard chapel overlooking the ocean, both testify to something greater! They are not an end in themselves, and regardless of their tourist value, their true value lies in their purpose—to be landmarks of faith. Joshua's memorial stones weren't individually remarkable, yet they created a remembrance spot for God's people. When people saw it, they would remember: *God brought us through the river!* The earth is covered with places where people have met the Lord and built a testimony with the hope that others would have an experience with Him like theirs.

The landmarks of our faith can be both tangible and intangible and are easily recognizable to our friends, neighbors, and acquaintances. God has called us to be salt that adds flavor to and preserves the world through a godly lifestyle. We are a light in a world that knows so much darkness. The world is desperate to find something that will give them hope and lead them to a love that will change their lives forever. How many times have you seen an advertisement that says, "This exercise program will change your life" or "This seminar will change your life" or "This event will change your life"? The programs sell, the seminars fill up, and the events are well attended because people are hungry for a life-changing experience. But only the Lord Jesus Christ can bring real change to a life through His saving power.

As Christians, we need to let others understand that we will encounter no obstacle that God cannot work in and help us overcome. He'll part the flooded river waters if necessary. We must show other people that a life of faithfulness has its rewards and that a life dedicated to the will of God brings fulfillment and true contentment. People will observe you during adverse circumstances to see what you are made of—to see what kind of God you serve and how you respond to Him. In a world that has seen too many pretenders, being real about God's character and work in your life is powerful.

> **We will encounter no obstacle that God cannot work in and help us overcome.**

During and After: Joshua's Example

Joshua set up a memorial in the middle of the Jordan River *during* Israel's deliverance (Josh. 4:9). Then he set up another memorial at Gilgal *after* Israel's deliverance from their enemies (v. 20). In a similar way the Holy Spirit encourages us not to wait until everything is over before building a memorial. In fact, we can build it while we are going through the situation. That's a step of faith! I don't have to wait for an answer to my prayer to start praising and thanking God. I can praise and thank God in advance; I can start shouting right now in faith because I know He is faithful.

So go ahead. No matter what you're going through, follow Joshua's example by building a memorial to God with stones of faith, prayer, praise, and worship.

If you could visit my office you would see "memorials" collected across the years that remind me of God's faithfulness to me in and through specific situations. Some of my memorials are pictures of faraway places where God met me in a special way and did something that I will never forget. Other memorials are physical objects that serve to remind me of His intervention—a piece of petrified wood, a stone, an alabaster box that contains items from a mission trip, a framed poem from my father when I was going through a difficult time that became God's "now" word to me.

To someone else my memorials probably look like odds and ends or even junk. But not to me. Each item has a spiritual connection with me, and when I look at it, I am reminded to thank God for His goodness, love, and mercy. When I look at it, I am transported back in time to the very place where He intervened or answered prayer.

You will have different reminders of places where you encountered God in a new and profound way. These are memorials that you can build, gather, or make to remind you of what God has done.

By erecting a landmark to God's faithfulness *during* a trial, *during* a difficult time, or *during* a puzzling situation, your faith and actions will effectively say, "I know, God, that You're going to see me through and bring me out on the other side abounding in a harvest of victory!" Doing this builds spiritual muscle and hushes the lies of the enemy.

Then *after* your victory comes, *after* the answer to prayer surfaces, *after* His intervention changes the situation, build another memorial of thankfulness to Him. And begin by using the stones of faith you used to build the first memorial. Go ahead and build another memorial and another and another. Before something else sidetracks you, build a memorial to the Lord. Before you have a second thought, remember what God has done for you first. Before you return to your routine, give Him the glory He deserves. After all, He is with you always, before, during, and after any difficult situation. God has been faithful to us; may we always be faithful to Him.

The journey *is* the reward.

Chinese Proverb

Encountering God Today

1. Without memory triggers, we tend to forget the goodness and power of the Lord God on our behalf. Why is it so important to remember what the Lord has done in your life?

2. When looking back over a life of faithfulness to the Lord and His Word, we should see miles of memorials to God's faithfulness, thousands of instances when God's love and mercy intervened. Write down some specific events in your life that have been a testimony to God's love and faithfulness.

3. As we have opportunity, we need to return to the places of our past—especially those significant to our faith—to remember God's goodness, His faithfulness, and the history of His answering our prayers. What places would you like to return to today? Which ones would you take your children to?

4. We must show other people that a life of faithfulness has its rewards and that a life dedicated to the will of God brings fulfillment and true contentment. How do your friends and neighbors view you currently? How do you want them to see you?

7

TRUST IN THE NAME
OF JESUS

Finding Strength
through Your Infirmity

Acts 3:1–10

It was cold and raining as my wife and I made our way through the darkened side streets of one of Paris, France's, arrondissements. Our goal was to find our hotel without getting soaked! From doorway to doorway we dodged our way in and out of every opening, seeking places of shelter.

As we entered one particular doorway, an old woman was huddled in the corner trying to keep warm. We had noticed her begging from passersby hours earlier on our way to dinner. Something in her eyes touched my heart as I asked God silently what he would have us do. We smiled at her and moved down the street to the next doorway.

I told my wife I sensed that the Lord wanted us to do something. She felt the same way. My wife waited for me as I made my way back up the street to find the old woman. She looked a bit shocked to see me again so quickly and may have thought I meant her harm. Nevertheless, in the best elementary French that I could muster, I explained to her that God loved her and saw her need and wanted me to give her something to encourage her and remind her that He cares. Gently I took her hand and placed in her palm the amount of money God had instructed me to give. As she began to count it, she began to sob uncontrollably and told me that she had been praying for a miracle so she could get by. I told her about God's greatest gift, Jesus, and then my wife and I headed back down the street.

For the next few mornings as we made our way to the Métro, we noticed that the doorway where she normally had been begging was vacant. We never saw her again. I'm sure our gift helped her out for a while, but it wasn't going to solve all her problems—only the Lord Jesus Christ could supply all of her need. We continued to pray for her.

Our experience that day in Paris reminds me of an experience Peter and John had shortly after Pentecost.

A Place Called Beautiful

Not long after the outpouring of the Holy Spirit on the day of Pentecost, Peter and John made their way to the temple for afternoon prayer. Acts 3 tells us they had an encounter with a crippled man who was lying in a place called "Beautiful." The main entrance to the temple area was called Beautiful Gate, and beautiful it was. An Alexandrian Jew named Nicanor designed the huge doors that made the Beautiful Gate. They were seventy-five feet high by sixty feet wide and made of Corinthian bronze, plated with gold and silver. These awesome doors were so heavy that it took the strength of twenty men to open and shut them. No expense was spared in creating the Beautiful Gate to the glory of God.

Although this place was called Beautiful and looked beautiful, in front of this particular gate were a myriad of people with a myriad of problems. The approaches to the temple were lined with sufferers of all kinds, begging for alms, seeking mercy, hoping that someone would take pity on them and their situation. The prime begging spots were those closest to the Beautiful Gate, which was essentially the door to God's presence. Surely this place called Beautiful, where people already had God on their mind, where people came ready to make a sacrifice, where people would be open to being more generous than usual, would be the most advantageous place to seek a handout. Thus the earlier a beggar arrived, the better his chance would be to lie all day long in a place called Beautiful.

You can be in a beautiful place and still have an ugly problem. Think about it. Adam and Eve were in the most beautiful place in the universe but had an ugly problem.

> You can be in a beautiful place and still have an ugly problem.

King Saul, King David, and King Solomon all lived in beautiful places, but they had some ugly problems that hindered them from being all they could have been for God. They and many others were just like this crippled man: stuck at the gate! Let's face it. There is nothing beautiful about being stuck in the same old place. It's discouraging to be in the same difficult place day after day, week after week, year after year. And it's disheartening to be surrounded by beauty but unable to enjoy it. It amounts to being a prisoner in the Promised Land.

Peter and John did not know the lame man's name. It's not recorded in Scripture. I have often wondered if his name was left out so that you and I could put our names there. Is this a story about us, about our spiritual condition, our situation? Maybe this man represents all of us. At one time or another, maybe now or maybe yesterday, we either are or were that poor man who was stuck at the gate. This hurting man was in a beautiful place with an ugly problem.

A misty morning does not signify a cloudy day.

Ancient Proverb

Comfortable in Our Infirmities

There are many people today with a spiritual condition comparable to that of the lame man at the Beautiful Gate. The unnamed man was more than forty years old. Think of that! For forty years he couldn't get beyond the gate. He could get to the gate, but he couldn't go through the gate. People could carry him to the gate, but that's all they could do for him.

The problem wasn't with the gate. Many people are stuck at the gate because of some problem. You can just imagine the approach to this huge gate filled with beggars seeking a handout. Although they may have had differing circumstances, once they were at the gate, they all had the same problem. They were stuck at the gate and unable to go any farther.

This scene paints a picture of the old adage, "Misery loves company." We all know that we can become almost comfortable in our unhappiness, comfortable with our pain and suffering, and even comfortable with our sinful ways. Our misery can become such a part of our lives and our own identities that we are no longer even conscious of it. We get used to being beaten down, accepting the lies of the enemy, speaking negatively about our situation rather than speaking the Word of God over it. The longer this goes on unchecked, the more it becomes a cyclical pattern that weaves its way into the fabric of our self-perception. In other words, we can't see ourselves healed and whole because we have so closely identified ourselves with our problems. Thus we can live in a beautiful place and still have an ugly problem that keeps us from moving ahead.

I am sure this particular crippled man got up that morning, just like a thousand other mornings, got dressed, and waited for his friends to come and help him to the place called Beautiful, where for the rest of the day he would sit and beg for alms. At the end of the day, his friends would come back by the temple to pick him up and carry him back home, where he would eat something, go to bed, and get up the next morning to do it all over again. That was his agenda, his life, all the poor man had ever known. I doubt that he ever got up and said to himself, *Today I'm going to find a new job, because I am not going to be crippled any longer.*

Many people are in a rut of doing the same thing day after day. They never get up and expect that day to be the one that will change their whole life. They never expect anything supernatural to happen to them. They never once think about a God in heaven who loves them so much that He would send someone their way with a message of hope and healing to turn their world upside down. God's Word asks, "How can they hear without someone preaching to them?" (Rom. 10:14 NIV). That "someone" must be us—the body of Christ. There are many people stuck at the door of the church, unable to get in because they have a problem that keeps them from moving forward with God. We must accept the responsibility to show them the way to trust God for their problem and move ahead in faith.

Many of us are stuck at the gate. We have become comfortable with an uncomfortable problem—the problem of depending too much on other people to meet our every need. When we're stuck at the gate, we have to depend on others. However, others can carry us only so far. People can't carry us into our God-designed destiny. We need something that will cause the crutches we've been depending on for so long to become unnecessary and useless. It's nice to have friends who will help us, and we should all be sensitive to the needs of those around us and those God puts on our hearts, but people should never be our main source of fulfillment. We must find that in the Lord.

When our need for people outweighs our need for God, we have a serious problem. Jesus wants to be and should be our Source, supplying every need. He is our Healer and our Guide. Listen and look around you. Is it possible that there's a voice or voices of those nearby who are God's voice to you, encouraging you to feed your faith on the Word of God? Does He want you to become more involved with other Christians so that they can nurture you in faith? I can remember times when I had a problem and found myself begging for things that would only dull my pain. Soon I found out, like the crippled man in the Acts story, that Jesus loves me very much and has ways I can't even imagine to meet my need. Whether through a song, a Scripture, someone praying for us, or just the counsel of a friend, His grace can reach us, bringing us help and health.

> When our need for people outweighs our need for God, we have a serious problem.

Healed

As the lame man saw Peter and John approaching him, no doubt he expected a monetary blessing that would help him get through the next day. Yet Peter and John wanted to offer him something that would get him through a lifetime—even an eternity! Peter said, "Look at us. . . . Silver and gold I do not have, but what I do have I give you: In the name of Jesus Christ of Nazareth, rise up and walk" (Acts 3:4, 6). Peter took him by his right hand and pulled him to his feet. Apparently his infirmity was in his feet and ankles, as the Bible says "immediately his feet and ankle bones received strength" (v. 7). The man could hardly believe it. He began to walk, and then he began to jump, and then he began to praise the Lord for his healing.

When Peter told him to trust in the name of Jesus for his healing, he never hesitated; he didn't think it over; he didn't look around for his friends to see what they thought. He knew this was no ordinary handout. He'd never been offered this before, and he let his faith go and simply believed. No doubt sitting where he sat day after day, he had heard of Jesus; he very well may have seen Jesus from a distance, but this day, this wonderful day, Jesus Christ changed his life forever. More valuable than any gift he'd ever received, more precious than all the gold and silver in the world, far beyond his wildest dreams, Jesus Christ met this troubled man in a place called Beautiful.

Thank God for Peter and John's boldness. Perhaps they had passed this man before and even given him something, but this time the Holy Spirit told them to give him a more valuable gift. Though he asked for coins, he needed a cure.

Jesus has given His followers authority to use His name, invoke His power, and declare His lordship over everything. He always backs up His name. Peter and John took Jesus at His word, and the lame man took them at their word. When we step out in faith and do what Jesus asks of us, He responds with the answer to our prayer for help.

This man had no thought of seeking God's mercy, but he received it that day. His healing was total and complete. There were no signs of weakness or stiffness in his limbs. Immediately this man showed himself strong and vigorous as if he'd never been crippled a day in his life. Forty years of being carried or using crutches were over. He would never have to sit at the gate again. In fact, as soon as he was healed, he walked through that gate called Beautiful for the first time and entered the temple courtyard on his own two feet.

God continues to meet seemingly impossible needs today. He can meet *your* need anytime and anywhere. Jesus heals so completely that once you have experienced it, you will not recognize the old you. The man's cure had not been effected by any power he had or even the power of John or Peter; his cure came by way of the power of Jesus Christ of Nazareth. Peter said, "In the name of Jesus Christ of Nazareth, rise up and walk!" (v. 6).

Jesus's wonderful name represents all that He is. When we have faith in His name, we have faith in His power and authority to answer our need and help us in any situation. Faith in this "name . . . above every name" (Phil. 2:9) is the avenue through which God works wonders in our lives. Trusting in His name can get us unstuck. Whether it's a difficult problem, a recurring sin, habits that seem to bind us to defeat, or a lifelong battle with a weakness, trusting in the name of Jesus for deliverance is the answer.

Faith in His name can be expressed in various ways. Acting on our faith is what is required. Maybe it's stopping the excuses and attending church. Maybe it's reading the Bible and allowing God's Spirit to speak truth to your heart. Maybe it's joining a small group of other believers who have been where you are and are working through their situation by admitting they need God's help to change. For the lame man it was grabbing the hand of Peter to get up. What "hand" is God extending to you? What is He asking you to do so that you can be healed or delivered and move on?

> You breathed Your fragrance upon me . . . and in astonishment I drew my breath . . . now I pant for You! I tasted You, and now I hunger and thirst for You. You touched me!—and I burn to live within Your peace.
>
> St. Augustine

Receiving the Strength to Move On

Beyond the lame man's healing is the bigger picture of what he did with the rest of his life. The last glimpse we have is of him standing beside Peter and John as they addressed the Sanhedrin, who rebuked them for healing this man. The Bible says that these religious leaders were dumbfounded when they saw the healed man, for they all recognized him and could hardly believe their eyes. This man who had lain at the gate of the temple for forty years was now inside giving his testimony. He had received the strength to move on. Jesus didn't heal him so he could come back the next day and beg again for alms. He healed him so that he could get on with God's plan for his life. And the same is true for us.

Many people have sat at the doors of the church for years, having been carried there by others. Many have lived off the scraps and pity of others. But is that really living? Is that all there is to this life? It's an existence far below what God intends for each one of us. Jesus died to give you and me a life that is overflowing, fruitful, and filled with love, joy, and peace. Just because I was raised in the church and know the lingo, that doesn't have anything to do with my salvation. Only Jesus can heal us, save us, and set us free from whatever it is that has contributed to and caused the crippled condition of our souls. People and things cannot do that.

What cripples you today? Are you tired of having to depend on people to get you to where you need to be spiritually? The lame man that we've been talking about had a little problem—it was his ankles. It's funny how a little problem can make the rest of your life miserable. What cripples you today? What problem is it that prevents you from moving ahead? Is it pride, greed, lust? Is it unforgiveness or bitterness from the past that you've allowed to dictate the course of your life? Maybe something that happened long ago has left an open wound that needs to be healed. The man in our story lay begging at the temple door for more than forty years. Each of us has a choice. We can scrape by on meager spiritual resources or we can allow God to bring change and growth. Are you in a beautiful place with an ugly problem? The Healer is on His way!

Maybe right now you're in a place where you feel stuck and unable to move forward in your own strength. You might even wonder, *Is there a right place to be for me to be healed of my condition?* There is, and it's right where you are. In the middle of your stuck condition, right in the middle of your crippled state, right where you are is where the Lord will meet you—only trust in His name for what you need. Let the past go, all the confusion, all the hurt, all the frustration, and go ahead and worship the Lord Jesus. Go ahead and praise Him. Go ahead—jump for joy and thank Him for healing your condition. Receive *now* the strength to go on, the strength to follow, and the strength to trust! The road to your healing begins with grabbing His hand and putting one foot in front of the other. Begin to thank and praise Him now. Begin to declare His promises. Rise up and move in the power of His Name!

May you *live* all the days of your life!

Jonathan Swift

Encountering God Today

1. If you were physically handicapped, for what aspects of your life would you have to depend on the help of others? Try to imagine the shame but necessity of having to beg for handouts just to get by. How would you feel about yourself?

2. The lame man's name is not mentioned in Scripture, perhaps so we can picture ourselves in the story. Are there aspects of his life that you can compare to your own in a spiritual sense? Have you ever been in a beautiful place with an ugly problem?

3. Peter and John speak the word of healing boldly and instruct the lame man to rise and walk in the name of Jesus. As Christians, what can we learn from their bold example? How should we respond to people in circumstances that seem impossible? Do you believe there's power in Jesus's name?

4. Are there areas in your life where you feel "stuck at the gate"? If so, what are they? Are you ready to fully trust in the name of Jesus and receive the strength to begin your journey into the things God has destined and designed you for? If so, pray right now and receive His healing mercy, love, and grace that are able to lift you up.

8

OFFER A SACRIFICE OF PRAISE

Discovering a Heart of Giving

2 Samuel 24:1–25; 1 Chronicles 21:1–28

All that hinders the Life from growing in us we must take away and keep away. That is our part.

Andrew Murray

Regifting has become a popular custom during the holiday season. Regifting means wrapping up a gift you received previously and giving it to someone else. Just be careful to change the name on the tag! I guess regifting works, but my conscience would bother me a bit—at least I hope it would. Regifting items isn't necessarily wrong, but it does cause the giver to miss out on experiencing the joy that comes from giving a gift that required sacrifice, thought, and love.

For instance, if I passed something off on Christmas Eve to a family member, and that person threw her arms around me to thank me for her "this-is-what-I-always-wanted" gift, the gratitude would make me feel like a louse. Not having paid for the gift, I couldn't fully appreciate giving the gift. It cost me nothing; thus, all I did was transfer it to someone else. Since the gift required little thought and no expense on my part, I would have trouble appreciating the joy of the one receiving it.

The Cost of Sacrifice

There are hundreds of passages in the Bible that deal with sacrifice. One of my favorites is in 2 Samuel, from the life of King David. In this account we find timeless truths about obedience, trust, and of course, the cost of sacrifice. The story takes place at the end of King David's reign, following a long and illustrious life as prophet, priest, and king to God's people, Israel. His combined ministry was a foreshadowing of the Messiah to come, Jesus Christ.

David was old and was now preparing his son Solomon to take over the leadership of the kingdom. For some reason, David was tempted to number his fighting men. In 1 Chronicles, where this same story is recorded, it says, "Satan stood up against Israel, and moved David to number Israel" (21:1). David could have resisted the temptation, but even after his military commander reminded David that this would show a lack of faith in God, David wanted the census (vv. 3–4). The nature of David's sin was probably pride, expressed in his leadership of a powerful and numerous people, and in his self-exaltation and boasting of his great accomplishments and strength. David was glorying in human ability and a great number of soldiers rather than in God's power and righteousness. Obviously David was proud of how many soldiers he had.

The Lord took offense at this census, or numbering of fighting men, because it showed that David trusted more in the strength of his army than in the strength of his God. This angered the Lord God, and like all sin, there was a heavy price to pay.

It took almost ten months to do the census—ten months in which David could have halted the count. However, when his commander Joab returned to give the report, he barely got the numbers out of his mouth when King David was stricken with guilt and remorse. He said, "I have sinned greatly in what I have done; but now, I pray, O LORD, take away the iniquity of Your servant, for I have done very foolishly" (1 Sam. 24:10).

At dawn's first light, a prophet named Gad came to King David with a message from the Lord. God was angry with David and with Israel, apparently for the nation's disobedience as well. God gave David the choice of what shape the punishment for his sin would take: three years of famine or three months of being pursued and overtaken by Israel's enemies or three days of plague in the land. I don't know about you, but I wouldn't want door number one, door number two, or door number three.

David did not want to fall into the hands of his enemies, so a plague came and wiped out seventy thousand men in three days. David was heartsick as he saw the death angel over Jerusalem. He fell on his face before God and said, "Was it not I who commanded the people to be numbered? I am the one who has sinned and done evil indeed; but these sheep, what have they done? Let Your hand, I pray, O Lord my God, be against me and my father's house, but not against Your people that they should be plagued" (1 Chron. 21:17).

David knew all too well that as a leader his sin was greater than the sin of the people. In concern for them, he was ready to accept all the punishment. One of David's best character traits was his willingness to be humble and accept God's punishment for his misdeeds.

> It's nothing against you to fall down flat; but to lie there—that's a disgrace.
>
> E. V. Cooke

A Place of Sacrifice

David had a trusted spiritual advisor and friend named Gad whom the Lord used in his life. As David was repenting and people were dying across the land, Gad made his way to the palace to visit the king with a prophetic word. Gad told David that he needed to build an altar to the Lord and sacrifice to Him right away (2 Sam. 24:18). Even in the midst of the calamity that was going on, in the midst of death and dying, tears and sorrow, he was to offer up a sacrifice of praise to God!

With a heavy heart, David set out for a threshing floor on Mount Moriah—the place Gad told him to go. The significance of this place is found in the fact that it was the exact spot where, on hearing David's prayers of repentance, God had stopped the destroying angel from taking further action (v. 16). God does hear and respond to our prayers for forgiveness. Thus David journeyed to the place where his intercession had made a difference. Later, under the reign of his son Solomon, the temple of the Lord would be built on this very spot.

A man named Ornan, also called Araunah, owned the threshing floor, and as he watched David approach, he realized it was the king. Running out to meet him, he fell at his feet and offered the king whatever he desired. David said he wished to buy the man's property and asked the price. Instead of naming a price, Ornan wanted to give his property, livestock, and even wood to the king. Then David said something that is a valuable lesson on worship for us: "I will not take what is yours for the Lord, nor offer burnt offerings with that which costs me nothing" (1 Chron. 21:24).

David paid full price for his sacrifice because he knew that *worship that costs nothing is worth nothing*! Had he taken the property and oxen as a gift and then in turn given it to the Lord, it would have cost him nothing. Therefore, it would not have been a sacrifice to God. A sacrifice is *not* a sacrifice unless it costs you something!

> A sacrifice is *not* a sacrifice unless it costs you something!

King David's words express the truth that—to God—the true value of our gifts, service, and lives is measured primarily by the sacrifice and cost involved. It's easy to praise Him when everything is going great, it's easy to thank the Lord when you're on the heights of a great victory, but there in the heat of the battle, when things are difficult and you don't know how you'll make it—that's when a sacrifice of praise opens the floodgates of God's mercy and love.

The Heart of Giving: Sacrifice

Unless our giving costs us something, it is hardly a sacrifice. When it comes to sacrificing to the Lord, as David did, there are three things that seem most important:

1. We should give God our best. I remember years ago someone using an expression that stopped me dead in my tracks: "The greatest enemy of best is good." I remember asking the Lord

to forgive me for all the times I had withheld my best from Him and offered Him something less.

2. A true sacrifice must be on God's terms—what He requires. I cannot have someone else sacrifice for me as if there were worship proxies. No! I need to trek up the mountain on my own, pay my own way, build my own altar, and offer myself on it. Only I can come before Him in brokenness and humility and awe, bearing a gift of praise that costs me something. It will cost you to say, "I praise you, Jesus," when you're going through a tough time. It's not easy to say, "Thank you, Lord, for everything," when it seems all is crumbling at your feet. It's a sacrifice to raise your hands in surrender to Him when the weight of the battle is on your shoulders. That's a sacrifice of praise! That's an offering of worship, coming from a heart that has found favor with God.

3. We must learn that circumstances change but God does not. He is worthy of praise when the sun is shining and when it's raining. He deserves my very best at all hours. In all things I must give Him thanks. By doing so, I am released from the bondage of living life based on circumstances. I begin to process life in the power of the Lord as my worship establishes a base of operation for Him to move and have His way.

> Worship is giving God the best that He has given you.
>
> Oswald Chambers

As much as I hate to admit it, and probably you do too, we've all tried to pull a fast one on the Lord. *Well, let's see, God said He wanted something; let me take a look around here and see what I'm not using that He can have.* It sounds terrible, doesn't it? Yet we've all done it. God doesn't do paper drives! He never calls us up the night before to say, "Just leave any items you don't want on the front porch and I'll pick 'em up while you're at church." God has never regifted us with anything. He gave us His best, Jesus Christ, who in turn gave us His best as well, His very life. And we try to get away with giving the King of Kings and the Lord of Lords whatever is lying around that we're not using! We've all done it, you know: given God the loose change in the car cup holder, had five-minute devotions so we could catch the game on TV, or volunteered for only those things that all of our friends are volunteering for.

Like King David, we should not accept free rides when it comes to giving and sacrificing to the Lord. We give our money to the Lord—that costs us something. And God has promised us that with the measure we use to give to Him, He'll measure it right back in blessing. God has promised to meet all of our needs if we'll bring the whole tithe into His storehouse: that is, 10 percent of our income. We are blessed when we give!

We give our time to the Lord—that costs us something. Where would the ministry of His church be if people did not volunteer their time and effort? The church has moved forward through the years because everyday folks sacrifice their time and talents to share His gospel, help the needy, clothe the naked, feed the hungry, teach a Sunday school class, and many other kinds of service. When we give our time to serve others, we bring a blessing to the Lord as well as to our own lives.

In the story about David, it says that he built his own altar to the Lord—he didn't bring in a building crew; he never appointed a committee to do it; he didn't ask for volunteers. He built it himself (1 Chron. 21:26). We should follow his example. We shouldn't ask someone else to build our altar for us. We should do it ourselves. We need to build our own place of sacrifice and once built, we need to climb up on top of it and sacrifice ourselves.

Total Surrender

When we offer ourselves daily to the Lord, it shows God we are serious about our commitment to Him and that He can count on us. It is a continual reminder that we're going to worship Him at all costs—come what may. During David's reign, there was peace, prosperity, and military success in Israel. The problem was that the Israelites (including David) forgot that this all came about because of the goodness of the Lord. Thus David and the people began to be proud and self-centered, and God punished them for their sin. We must guard against such attitudes by coming daily to the Lord and humbly offering Him all that we have.

We used to sing this song in church when I was a child:

> All to Jesus I surrender,
> All to Him I freely give;
> I will ever love and trust Him,
> In His presence daily live.
> I surrender all, I surrender all.
> All to Thee, my blessed Savior,
> I surrender all.
>
> Judson W. Van DeVenter

This is what David's actions on Mount Moriah meant that day: *I surrender all!* We must come to the place where we find our strength and security only in God and not in people, might, possessions, fame, success, money, position, or any other thing. If we were to lose all that we have, what would we have left? We would have only the Lord, and He is enough. Only He is worthy of our praise. Life's security and significance need to be rooted and grounded in our relationship with Jesus.

As you look around our world today, you do not have to look too far to see everyday men and women offering up a sacrifice of praise. I have both met and read stories of people who serve the Lord gladly in the midst of adversity, persecution, and physical challenge. Many suffer throughout the earth for the sake of the gospel, but they do so with great joy. Missionaries, Bible translators, Christian educators, Bible smugglers, pastors, aid workers, and others fearlessly offer up a sacrifice of praise as they face great risk every day. They do it because they know, as David did, that whatever reality we are functioning in, whatever our situation may be, God is above and beyond it all. He alone transcends our reality and makes His presence known. And in His presence we experience endless love, great compassion, and all-sufficient grace.

Mother Teresa, a small, frail, Albanian Roman Catholic nun, won the hearts of millions with her sacrifice of praise. Choosing to live among some of the world's poorest people in India, she radiated God's love into the muck and mire of suffering. Whenever you saw her, she was smiling, always happy, always full of the joy of the Lord, and always giving praise to God. Her whole life was offered up as a sacrifice of praise as she preferred others above herself and made her home with society's outcasts. She is just one of many who daily choose to offer up a sacrifice of praise no matter the situation they find themselves in. Their lives remind us of the importance of giving God our very best and not being ashamed to praise Him loud and long! By doing so, we keep in the forefront of our hearts and minds that all blessing comes through God and not from our own efforts.

All that we have are gifts from God, and we should use them for His glory and not for generating personal pride. When it comes to blessing Him, He desires that we hold nothing back. The best gift we can give Him is the gift of ourselves. He delights in our sacrifice of praise; in our willing worship, based on who He is and not on what we feel like; and our thanksgiving in the midst of any trial, because we know in our heart that in Him is deliverance and victory. Praise the Lord!

Encountering God Today

1. God had blessed David above and beyond anything he ever could have imagined, and yet David took his eyes off the Blesser and focused on the blessing. Have you ever been tempted to put your faith and trust in what you own, whom you know, or what you've accomplished rather than in the One who has blessed you? If so, when?

2. Scripture makes it clear that David's sin adversely affected the lives of many others. What are the ways in which your sin affects those around you? What steps can you take to make sure that you don't yield to temptation?

3. When David felt the convicting power of the Lord in regard to his sin, he quickly began to repent and seek God's forgiveness. How do you respond to the voice of the Holy Spirit when He points out the error of your ways?

4. King David refused to accept the offer of the threshing floor and animals as a gift. He said, "I will not make an offering to the Lord with that which costs me nothing!" What can we learn from this? Why is it important to offer our own sacrifice of praise to the Lord?

9

THANK THE LORD

Cultivating a Heart of Gratitude

Luke 17:11–19

Have you ever done something special for someone and received no acknowledgment? It may have been a present you sent or a surprise you planned. It stings when there is no response. Ingratitude is probably one of the worst social blunders we can commit; it is just wrong not to take the time to say thank you.

Sometimes we forget to say thanks because we get so caught up in the gift we have received. For instance, when children open a birthday or Christmas present, they are often so thrilled that they forget what's supposed to come next. Then parents remind them,

"What do you say? Shouldn't you thank Grandma and Grandpa?"

Beyond poor social graces, not saying thank you shows a lack of respect and insensitivity to the gift giver and—if allowed to go unchecked—will cause callousness and indifference to the love of others and leave one stagnant and selfish. On the spiritual plane of our lives, ingratitude to God is certainly a sin, and it must grieve Him when we fail to thank Him for His bountiful gifts.

On a daily basis I practice quoting Psalm 34:1—"I will bless the LORD at all times; His praise shall continually be in my mouth." Every day, rain or shine, comfort or pain, in good times and bad, I let Him know that I am going to bless Him, extol Him, honor Him, praise Him, worship Him, thank Him—come what may—because He's still God no matter what's going on in my life. There is always something to thank and praise Him for, and He is pleased when we thank Him before, during, and after every circumstance, test, or trial in our lives. He is the one constant through it all. He will never leave us or forsake us.

When it is hard to find something to praise God for, I quote Scripture; it causes me to be thankful for His Word, for it is life to me.

When it comes to spiritual gratitude, it was on the cross where Jesus, in His cruel death, suffered the lowly ingratitude of man in all of its fullness. Just prior to the days of His suffering, He experienced a measure of the ingratitude of man when He encountered ten lepers. Their story, like so many in Scripture, mirrors our own and reminds us of the importance of saying thank you to the Lord.

Ten Lepers Healed

Making His way to Jerusalem through the regions of Samaria and Galilee, Jesus arrived in a village where ten lepers, appropriately standing away from everyone else, shouted to Him from a distance, "Jesus, Master, have mercy on us!" (Luke 17:13). There are several things at play here in their cry for mercy, telling us the lepers knew quite a bit about Jesus of Nazareth. First, they knew He had the power to heal. Second, they knew His mercy was without limit. And third, they knew He was their only hope. The text doesn't tell us how long they had suffered with this terrible disease, but their distance indicates that they were societal outcasts and literally cut off from the rest of society. Their existence was horrific both physically and mentally.

According to Leviticus and the Law, lepers were not allowed to live with anyone except other lepers. They were required to live away from the populated places in total isolation from all (Lev. 13:46). Imagine never being able to hold your children, hug a loved one, or feel an arm of comfort around your shoulders. Furthermore, lepers were required to announce their infection to all who came near by calling out, "Unclean, unclean." Talk about being ostracized! There was simply no escaping their wretched condition. Thus it is little wonder that when they heard Jesus was coming, their hearts must have welled up inside them, for His reputation had preceded Him.

On hearing their cries for mercy, Jesus simply said, "Go, show yourselves to the priests" (v. 14). This was what the Law required (Lev. 14:3–4). He spoke no word of healing and never touched them, but He met their deepest need. As they obeyed, as they honored His words and did what He said, their healing came. Not one of them was healed until he obeyed. They were cleansed as they went. They may not have understood what had happened, but they had faith in Jesus's authority and did what He said.

I am sure that they were absolutely shocked at first. Was it the feeling inside that told them a miracle was taking place, or did they look down at their arms and legs and notice that the sores, discoloration, and lesions were gone? The miracle came about because they took Jesus at His word. They didn't question or complain, just acted on His command.

What a lesson for us! Would we see greater things in our lives if we obeyed all that He told us? God's Word says that He honors obedience more than sacrifice (1 Sam. 15:22).

This is powerful. As the lepers walked away, something wonderful happened. The very power of God infused their diseased bodies and brought newness of life to every fiber of their being—literally! They were made whole as they obeyed Jesus by going to the priests. With each step, they received strength for the next and the next and the next. One can't help but imagine what the priests' reaction must have been when they arrived with skin that was clean and smooth. No doubt the priests knew them as lepers, and no doubt they were amazed when they saw them with no open wounds, no lesions, and no discolored blotches. A miracle of God had taken place.

> Whatever comes from the heart carries the heat and color of its birthplace.
>
> Oliver Wendell Holmes

The Gratitude of One

Somewhere in the midst of the wonderment of it all, the thoughts of one of the healed lepers returned to the One who had healed him. He decided to go back and say thank you to Jesus. "Now one of them, when he saw that he was healed, returned, and with a loud voice glorified God, and fell down on his face at His feet, giving Him thanks. And he was a Samaritan" (Luke 17:15–16).

When God does something amazing, it is difficult to keep quiet about it. "With a loud voice" this leper praised the Lord. It must have pleased Jesus to hear this man express gratitude for his healing. He came all the way back to the place of God's mercy, where his need had been met. He ran back, perhaps hoping that Jesus was still around, wanting to connect with the Healer one more time.

As wonderful as all of this is, there is another part of the story that we must address: where are the other nine that were healed? All ten cried out for God's mercy and received it. All ten were healed as they obeyed the Master. All ten presented themselves to the priests and were pronounced "clean." And yet only one man thought to go back and say thank you. Only one gave immediate gratitude for immediate healing. This one cleansed man turned to Jesus; the other nine turned their backs and walked away. They didn't just walk away—they walked away healed and whole, forgetting the One who had made it all possible. Oh, how their ingratitude must have hurt the heart of the Lord!

After receiving the praise and worship of the healed Samaritan, Jesus said, "Were there not ten cleansed? But where are the nine? Were there not any found who returned to give glory to God except this foreigner?" (vv. 17–18). The ingratitude must have stung our Lord. He had saved the lives of ten men, but only one expressed his gratitude. And Jesus remarked that the worship and thanksgiving that did come were from the lips of a foreigner—considered by locals to be nothing more than a dog. The worship of this "dog," however, teaches us all a lesson: gratitude and goodness flow from inside. Being grateful and gracious comes from character, not race or ethnicity. It emanates from the posture of our hearts and the realization that only God is responsible for any good in our lives.

> Being grateful and gracious comes from character, not race or ethnicity. It emanates from the posture of our hearts and the realization that only God is responsible for any good in our lives.

There is something haunting about Jesus's words, "But where are the nine?" The ten men were a group when they had leprosy. After their healing, however, their individual responses set them apart. This story should trouble us, because many times we have been among the nine who have sought God's mercy and grace, received it, and gone on with life, happy for the blessing but never stopping to let Him know. We remember God in our need but forget Him in our abundance. One in ten—are the odds any different today? Probably not. Does it hurt the Lord any less? I'm sure not.

What should we do with the blessing, favor, grace, mercy, and love we receive? Return it! Yes, return it to the One who made it all possible and return it in kind to those around us in this world. We need to cultivate a heart of thanksgiving, beginning with daily praising and thanking the Lord for each blessing. Every time we say, "Thank You, Jesus," "Praise You, Lord," or "I love You, God," it shows God that we appreciate all He has done, is doing, and is yet to do in our life. Jesus died not only to save us from our sins but to reestablish relationship between humankind and our Maker. What we lost in the Garden of Eden, Jesus brought back through the cross: relationship. When we have a relationship with Him, we will remember to give Him thanks.

Taking a Gift for Granted

God continues to bless us on a daily basis, but do we thank Him daily? Do we give thanks only for the "big-ticket items"? Should we not thank Him for our daily provisions? We rob the heart of God of great joy when we fail to say thank you. Cultivating a heart of thanksgiving will also cultivate in us a heart of compassion and open us up to even greater blessing.

Ungratefulness sours the blessings in our lives and dams the flow of what God can do in and through us. Ingratitude denies God the glory due His great name. He is worthy of our praise whether He's "done something" for us or not. He is God, and beside Him there is no other! He is God all by Himself. He who flung the stars in place and spun the planets into their orbits is worthy of all glory and honor! The Giver is more important than any gift He's given to us.

Gratitude unlocks the floodgates of blessing into our lives. Ingratitude keeps us mumbling and complaining, judgmental and jealous, selfish and self-centered. Ingratitude is really a heart posture that says, "I deserve to be blessed." Our own society today is filled with talk of everyone's individual rights and how we must protect them. In this atmosphere it's easy to become full of ourselves and not too concerned about anyone else. We spend far more time pleading than we do praising. We must not forget that Jesus died on a cross in our place. It wasn't right that He should suffer and die, but He did it because of His love for us. He did it for relationship. He did it because He wanted to offer us a better life and an eternity with Him.

Taking the gifts and blessings of God for granted puts us in a spiritually precarious place. Just how far do we think we can get by not being thankful to the Lord? How can we receive salvation but not be thankful for it? Psalm 50:23 says, "He who sacrifices thank offerings honors me, and he prepares the way so that I may show him the salvation of God" (NIV). Living a life of thankfulness keeps the channel of God's blessing and provision open. Acknowledging that every good and perfect gift comes from Him keeps our hearts in check and reminds us that no one is good except God alone.

> We spend far more time pleading than we do praising.

I don't know about you, but I want to "prepare the way" and get the clutter out of my life by lifting up a sacrifice of thanksgiving, by opening the channel for the river of God's Holy Spirit to work in my life. Having a grateful heart toward the Lord helps us continually mine the fields of our lives for even more things for which to give Him praise. Like a metal detector at the seashore that sounds the alarm when it hones in on an object buried beneath billions of grains of sand, so a grateful heart becomes more and more aware of God's many blessings. Within the context of each of our days, there are many things for which we can offer thanks to God.

Sometimes a light surprises the Christian when he sings; it is the Lord who rises with healing in His wings.

William Cowper

Thanksgiving at the Feet of Mercy

Gratitude fits us for greater blessing. God is always ready to give more abundantly when previous gifts are properly valued, appreciated, and enjoyed. And so many times, the added gift of joy and peace is far more precious than the material gift for which we have thanked Him. This is what the Samaritan in our story soon found out. When he went back to thank Jesus, he fell in worship at His feet. Jesus was moved with compassion and said, "Arise, go your way. Your faith has made you well" (Luke 17:19). Jesus wasn't talking about the man's physical health this time. He was talking about his spiritual well-being. In other words, He was saying, "Your faith has saved you!" This man, this foreigner, this Samaritan received the double cure that day. Not only did he receive physical healing at the Lord's command, but he received salvation—healing for his sin-sick soul. Wow!

Now we begin to see how the other nine missed out. Now we can understand why Jesus was so broken-hearted when they did not all return. He had *more to give.* He had more blessing in store. He had wanted to heal them inside as well as on the outside. We miss so much when we don't go back to say, "Thank You, Lord!" What great blessing do we forfeit by not returning to render praise? What eternal treasures do we surrender by not going back to the place of our deliverance and offering up a sacrifice of praise? Psalm 103:2 tells us: "Bless the Lord, O my soul, and forget not all His benefits." Remembering and counting our blessings are ways of showing God we are truly thankful.

Herbert Lockyer once said, "God always suffers more when ingratitude is shown by those who dwell beneath his shadows." Let us not be like the nine. Let us be like the one who cared enough to return and fall at the feet of Mercy and say thank you. We are privileged to live and dwell beneath the shadow of the Almighty. We are blessed to be able to call on the Lord at any time and in any circumstance. We are the richer for having received from His gracious hand the bounty that He has poured out on our lives. Should we not all fall at His feet and say, "All glory and honor belongs to You"? May our thanksgiving ascend to His ears as a precious gift. May our thanksgiving become an integral part of our nature as we say thank you often and with a loud voice.

> Therefore by Him let us continually offer the sacrifice of praise to God, that is, the fruit of our lips, giving thanks to His name. But do not forget to do good and to share, for with such sacrifices God is well pleased.
>
> Hebrews 13:15–16

Encountering God Today

1. Have you ever given someone a gift that he or she did not acknowledge? How did it make you feel? Did you care at all? If you're totally honest, did it make you wish just a little that you hadn't bothered in the first place?

2. You've heard the old adage, "Misery loves company." All ten lepers were together in their suffering, and yet once healed, they parted ways in terms of their response. What would your response have been? Would you have returned to look for Jesus? What makes the Samaritan's response so significant?

3. Most of us tend to pray that God will give us what we need more than we praise Him for answering our prayers. Do you think Jesus cares if we thank Him? Do you think it saddens Him when we don't take the time to tell Him how grateful we are for what He's done in our lives? If so, why?

4. Why is it important to return thanks? What does "cultivating a heart of thanksgiving" mean? Are you cultivating one? If not, how can you begin?

10

MAKE THE ULTIMATE SACRIFICE

Trusting God without Question

GENESIS 22:1–19

Courage is faith that has said its prayers.

Dorothy Bernard

The spring semester of my freshman year of college was a turning point in my life. I had entered school as a music major—gravitating to what was natural for me and never giving any thought to another field of study. Playing, performing, and competing in piano since grade school, I had always known that music would be my life and security. By now I was beginning to write my own songs and sing them as well. Music consumed my world and always had since I was about four-and-a-half years old, when I began to bang out tunes by memory on the piano.

I distinctly remember the Lord speaking to my heart about my music, not so much as a career choice but rather as a ministry for Him. Sure, I'd grown up singing in church and still did, but this was not what was being addressed to my spirit that spring.

The Lord's prodding began to actually frighten me a bit and made me nervous inside because the Holy Spirit was now using the "M" word: *ministry*! I never minded helping out or assisting in the cause—sign me up—but to actually and intentionally be called, trained for, and prepared for a lifetime of ministry was not on my agenda; apparently it was on God's. For the first time in my young life, I came face-to-face with my idea of what the future looked like and what God's idea of my future looked like, and they were not the same. Being in the ministry certainly didn't sound like fun, didn't sound prestigious or profitable, and where on earth was I going to end up now—the Amazon? I had to think this through. It was going to take a while. I told God I'd get back to Him in a few days—ha!

Soon my world came crashing down. I couldn't eat or sleep; I could barely pray. I was simply numb and knew that I would be in direct disobedience to the Lord if I were to say no to His call. But my disdain for the "M" word was fed by years and years of seeing the damage done by so-called Christians within the church—much of it inflicted on ministers and those in leadership. No thanks, I did not want to sign up for that kind of life. Who would want it? You have to be half out of your mind to want to go into the ministry. It was the most thankless job I could ever think of, and yet I knew what I must do. I really didn't have a choice if in fact the Lord was truly Lord of my life and not just a figurehead.

Thus, after days of agonizing and going back and forth in my head over it all, I finally knelt down before the Lord and basically said, "What is it You want me to do?" In the deafening silence, He spoke to my heart, telling me to get a sheet of paper and a pen and list everything that was important to me. I wrote and wrote: family, friends, physical and tangible blessings of all kinds. I placed it on the floor before Him. He told me that the list wasn't finished. I stared and stared at it and wondered what I had missed. I had omitted my future—music! What a self-discovery that moment was as I added that to the list and then said to the Lord, "If You want my music, You can have it. If You should require of me never to sing or play again, I won't." As tears streamed down my face, I knew then I had laid everything at His feet.

I stood up, put the piece of paper in one of my books, and walked outside with a deep sense of peace. It took me several weeks to process it all and to come to the realization that it wasn't my music or any of those things listed on the paper that God wanted—it was me! He wanted me! He wanted to know that I loved Him first and foremost, and I needed to know this as well, for my own spiritual benefit. If Jesus was truly to be Lord of my life, then that meant withholding nothing from Him. He sanctified—set apart—my music and gave it back to me with a call attached: minister His Word. The gifts that He had bestowed on me were to be used for His glory and not for the glory of anyone else.

The only way to Jesus is alone.

Anonymous

Obedience Is Better than Sacrifice

The Bible is full of examples of God's requiring something from individuals, though none, in my opinion, is as heartrending as when He called Abraham to sacrifice his son Isaac. Genesis 22:1–19 records the story of God's asking Abraham to offer his son—the son who was to be Abraham's future, his legacy, his son of promise, his security, the one whose birth was brought about by a miracle in Abraham and Sarah's old age. How could God, who had promised Isaac to them in the first place and brought about his birth, now require that their son's life be ended? None of this makes sense on the surface. And yet we all would agree that God's thoughts are not like ours, nor are His ways like our own (Isa. 55:8–9).

Abraham, Sarah, and Isaac were living in Beersheba when God interrupted the day-to-day routine, saying, "Abraham! . . . Take now your son, your only son Isaac, whom you love, and go to the land of Moriah, and offer him there as a burnt offering on one of the mountains of which I shall tell you" (Gen. 22:1–2). If Abraham had a verbal response, we are not told of it in Scripture. We are told only that early the next morning, he obeyed. His heart must have sunk within him. Furthermore, imagine Abraham putting on a brave face in front of both Sarah and Isaac as he began to gather things for the three-day journey so that they could go and "worship" God. His wife and son were worshipers as well and knew all too well that Abraham would go to any lengths to honor the Lord and obey His voice, but this . . . how in the world could He tell them this?

The day after receiving the Lord's instructions, Abraham saddled up his donkey and tied on wood for the offering. He took with him two trusted servants and Isaac. They journeyed for three days—three days of talking about the weather, their surroundings, current events, but not a word about what they were going to do. The young men had no idea what the plan was; they were just following their master, Abraham. Isaac, without a care in the world, trusted in his father's love for him. On the third day, Mount Moriah came into view, and no doubt its sight caused sorrow to fill every recess of Abraham's soul.

As they reached Moriah, Abraham's calm demeanor surely belied how he really felt. His mind must have been reeling in anguish over his boy.

Abraham instructed his servants to stay behind with the donkey while he and Isaac went further to worship God. Then he said something so profound that you might miss it if you're not careful: "The lad and I will go yonder to worship, and we will come back to you" (v. 5). Did you catch it? Abraham said, *"We'll come back to you!"*

I believe Abraham complied with the Lord's instructions because he knew the Lord. He knew the Lord's heart, and he knew that the Lord loved both him and Isaac. There had to be some underlying strength within his own heart that told him somehow, some way, in the end it would be okay and God would make it right. The God who had called him out of Ur, who had never let him down or failed him, who had provided for his every need, certainly would not change His nature now.

The apostle Paul tells us in his letter to the Romans that Abraham "did not waver in unbelief at God's promise, but was strengthened in his faith and gave glory to God, because he was fully convinced that what He had promised He was also able to perform" (Rom. 4:20–21 HCSB). Abraham loved the Lord so much and believed in the promises God had spoken over him and Isaac, that should Isaac have to die, Abraham believed that God would certainly raise him up. As Paul writes in that same chapter, "He [Abraham] believed in God, who gives life to the dead and calls things into existence that do not exist" (Rom. 4:17 HCSB). Either Abraham would become the father of many nations or God was a liar. And no doubt now, here at Moriah as he made his way to the summit with fire in one hand and a knife in the other and Isaac at his side carrying the very wood he would die on, his faith speaks to us down through the ages that God will make a way.

When Abraham and Isaac reached the summit, Abraham built an altar, arranged the wood on the altar, and then bound his son, placing him on top of the wood. As Abraham raised the knife to kill Isaac, immediately an angel of the Lord called out, "Abraham, Abraham!" and told him, "Do not lay your hand on the lad or do anything to him; for now I know that you fear God, since you have not withheld your son, your only son, from Me" (Gen. 22:11–12). God didn't want Isaac to be killed. God wanted to know that Abraham was His. Even after all this time, after everything they'd been through together, God wanted to know where Abraham's loyalties lay. Did Abraham value the blessing or the Blesser? Did he love the gifts in his life more than the Giver? This was heart-check time for the one through whom all nations would be blessed.

Samuel, the prophet, told us of the importance of our individual obedience to the Lord when he said, "Does the Lord delight in burnt offerings and sacrifices as much as in obeying the voice of the Lord? To obey is better than sacrifice" (1 Sam. 15:22 NIV). The example of Abraham's willingness to sacrifice Isaac embodies this passage of Scripture. It all comes down to obeying the voice of the Lord our God. Sometimes as we do what God has called us to do, we discover it has been a litmus test for our faith in and love for the Lord.

Those who know the path to God can find it in the dark.

Alexander Maclaren

God Will Make a Way

When there is no other way, God will make a way. Our story doesn't end with the angel of the Lord speaking God's directives. As Abraham no doubt breathed a sigh of relief and quickly untied his son, they noticed a ram caught by its horns in the thicket nearby. The ram, not Isaac, became the sacrifice. God had provided another way. In fact, Abraham declared that Moriah be called Jehovah-jireh, meaning, "The Lord Will Provide!" And God did, and God does provide for us today. His supply is sufficient in all things. When we obey Him and find that there is no way out, no other plan, no alternative, no door or window, take heart, for the Lord will provide. He will supply just what you need just when you need it.

Isaac's actions reveal more about his spiritual life than what little the text records. The only thing recorded that Isaac said is, "Father? . . . The fire and the wood are here, but where is the lamb for the burnt offering?" His dad replied, "God himself will provide the lamb for the burnt offering, my son" (see Gen. 22:7–8 NIV). You have to believe that Isaac was beginning to get the picture concerning what was going on here. And yet he became a willing partner in it all. Many scholars believe that Isaac was most certainly an adult by now and possibly even in his thirties. He could have taken his own father down for the count, shrugged off the entire event, and headed for home, but that's not what happened.

Isaac was a willing partner because he loved and believed in God and His promises, as his father did. There is no question that Abraham and Sarah had raised him in the fear and admonition of the Lord. Isaac's trust in his own father mirrors the trust Abraham had in his heavenly Father. The lessons learned at Moriah that day would serve Isaac the rest of his life. In addition, Isaac was there when the angel of the Lord spoke and reaffirmed God's promise: "Because you have done this and have not withheld your son, your only son, I will surely bless you and make your descendants as numerous as the stars in the sky and as the sand on the seashore. Your descendants will take possession of the cities of their enemies, and through your offspring all nations on earth will be blessed, because you have obeyed me" (vv. 16–18 NIV).

I'm sure that if others had known what Abraham was going to do, they would have called him crazy and restrained him with all force. And yet there are times in our lives when God calls us to do something or go somewhere that may in fact seem off the wall to others. We need to be concerned about pleasing the Lord rather than looking to others to validate what God is saying to us. God may ask you to give up something, and someone might say, "Oh, that's not God; that can't be God. He's never told me to do anything like that." But you see, you have to go to the mountain for yourself. No one else can do it for you. What God requires of you at this moment may not be what He's requiring of your neighbor. You can be responsible only for what the Lord is calling you to do with your life. Understandably, God will never tell us to do anything that isn't in accordance with His Word.

You may be wondering how you will be able to offer to God what He requires; you may think that you don't have it in you to follow through with His instruction. I want to encourage you today with this: be more concerned about being obedient than about whatever it is He's calling you to sacrifice. Just do it! Notice that neither Abraham nor Isaac complained; they complied. The Lord always rewards obedience, for it blesses His heart and assures Him of our loyalty and love. Follow through with whatever He calls you to do, and I guarantee that He'll provide whatever you need to make your service to Him complete.

The Ultimate Sacrifice

God will not call us to something that is not true of Himself. He always calls us to a place or to a path where, when it's all said and done, more of His likeness and character will be seen in us with the result that the flow of His blessing on our lives will be without limit. Hebrews 11:17–19 says:

> By faith Abraham, when he was tested, offered up Isaac, and he who had received the promises offered up his only begotten son, of whom it was said, "In Isaac your seed shall be called," accounting that God

was able to raise him up, even from the dead, from which he also received him in a figurative sense.

The entire account of Abraham's willingness to make the ultimate sacrifice of his son is surely a type and shadow that points to the future when God the Father offered His Son, Jesus Christ, as a sacrifice for the sins of all humankind.

Jesus, the Lamb of God, took our place on the altar of a cross centuries later—near the very spot where Abraham had offered Isaac. There was certainly no ram substitute for Jesus, as He became *our* sinless substitute, making the ultimate sacrifice on our behalf. Thus God demonstrates to each one of us that He will not withhold anything, even His only Son, so that we too may call Him "Abba, Father" and become heirs of the spiritual blessing that He makes possible through our Lord and Savior, Jesus the Christ (see Rom. 8:15–17).

With Jesus as our example, we come to understand the true meaning of obedience and sacrifice. In Him they fuse together as one and the same. For you and me it is all about surrender—spiritual surrender. Though my situation and calling to the ministry is in no way as extreme as what God required of Abraham, there are similarities for us all. For at one point or another, God will identify something in our lives that He wants us to surrender to Him. And I've lived long enough to tell you that it will, and does, happen again and again. At different stages in our lives and in our relationship with God, He may allow a test to come to reveal what is truly in our heart, to make sure that no person or thing is competing with Him for our affection. He desires that our heart be in alignment with His.

When God tested Abraham, He didn't want a sacrifice of Isaac. He wanted Abraham. And He wants you and me as well. With each test or trial we are given the opportunity to be obedient and to sacrifice so that God can release even greater blessing in our lives and entrust us with whatever He wants to give us. The Lord wants our full attention, and sometimes He has to go to great lengths to make sure He gets it. I'm glad He does. Once we get beyond the letting go part of it all, God is able to move in ways we never imagined before. He knows us best and knew us first and loves us like no other ever could. Usually we discover that through our sacrifice God is able to do something in our lives that is totally satisfying or fulfilling.

When I think of this, I am reminded of something Jesus said, which may not be easy to hear but is for our good: "Whoever of you does not forsake all that he has cannot be My disciple" (Luke 14:33). This isn't about not having nice things. Things are not God's concern unless those things begin to own you or me. The Lord is not going to share first place in our heart with anyone or anything. The Ten Commandments tell us to have no other gods before Him.

It has been years since the Lord called me to the ministry. Since then I've had many conversations with others who wrestled the same way I did when I heard God's voice. I wish I could have been like Abraham, gathering everything I needed and heading for my

Moriah, but that's not what happened. I went kicking and screaming. Abraham didn't complain; I did. Abraham never questioned; I did. But then, Abraham had been through some stuff by that point in his life, and God had a track record with him that was flawless. Looking back, I don't know why I was so uptight about my future or anxiously wondering what God was going to require of me or make me do. I realize now that He has called me to be childlike, not childish, in my response to His call. Childlike means I accept Him at His word and act on it, trusting in His love and care for me. And should I ever reach a place where I don't possess what is required, He will provide it for me to use for His glory.

Right now you may be headed to the summit of a mountain with fire in one hand and a knife in the other to kill the very thing that is near and dear to your heart, but God will meet you there. We can become so enamored with what we think our future or our security looks like that, without meaning to, we replace God in our heart with our dream. We can grow comfortable if we stay in the same place spiritually for a while, living life on autopilot in some kind of false predictability, but that's not God's will. His will is for our relationship with Him to be vibrant and dynamic, so that we are constantly learning, growing, and surrendering to Him. And should He ever call you to slay the very thing you love—such as a job, a position, some material possession, etc.—be willing to do it, because it means He has something greater in store for you.

Big purposes free us from petty fretfulness and little ailments.

Ralph Washington Sockman

The Blessing of Our Sacrifice

When Abraham laid his future—Isaac—on the line and proved to God that he was the kind of man He could depend on, it opened a fountain of blessing that still flows today. Ask yourself this question: *Who around me, in my life, will be blessed because of my obedience to the Lord?* You see, our obedience to God will always impact someone else—always. When God asks or requires something of me, my obedience will open the floodgates of blessing to my family, my children, and, in fact, my children's children, until the Lord comes back. Laying my will and my way on the altar now will have an impact long after I'm gone. God's Word is full of examples, page after page, where people were impacted generation after generation by a decision someone made long before the future generations ever drew breath.

Remember, God doesn't want something; He wants you! You are the reason He sent His Son to die and rise again from the dead. He wanted you to have life everlasting and live life to the full. God wants first place in your heart and my heart. When He calls us to the place of surrender, we must go or we will never be able to embrace our destiny or discover the future He had planned for us. Just think about it: what if Abraham refused to go to Moriah? What if?

I don't want to come down to the end of my days and wonder, *What if?* I want to know that I have been in His will. I want to experience all that He has for me. I want to live in such a way that His favor and blessing attend my life. And should He call me to sacrifice something in my life or give up some desire or some plan, it's okay, because He can resurrect anything He wants to. He loves us with an everlasting love that will never require of us anything apart from His ultimate best. "We know that all things work together for good to those who love God, to those who are the called according to His purpose" (Rom. 8:28).

It seems impossible that God would ask Abraham to sacrifice his son. Yet God was testing the depth of Abraham's love and devotion to Him. At some point in our lives, God may require us to give up to Him that which we love the most. He wants to test our willingness to be "all or nothing" worshipers. God does not mind that we have "things," He just doesn't want "things" to have us. God redeemed Isaac from the altar and honored Abraham's worship. He provided Abraham with the appropriate sacrifice and, in that moment, revealed His love—but only after Abraham had obeyed Him. Our hearts reveal how sinful and wayward we are, but when we come to God in repentance and seek His forgiveness, He provides the offering that sets us free through the blood of His own Son, Jesus Christ.

> Nothing You ask of me will harm me . . . though You want to put to death in me the selfish . . . the fearful . . . and all that keeps me from walking close to You.
>
> St. Francis of Assisi

Encountering God Today

1. When God's requests don't seem to make sense on the surface, why is it important to remember that His thoughts and His ways are not like ours (see Isa. 55:8–9)?

2. What is it about obedience that is so important to God? Why would He say in His Word: "Does the LORD take pleasure in burnt offerings and sacrifices as much as in obeying the LORD? Look: to obey is better than sacrifice" (1 Sam. 15:22 HCSB)?

3. When there is no other way, God will make a way. Why should we keep this in mind when the Lord calls us to lay something down or sacrifice something in our lives?

4. Our obedience to God will always impact others. Who is it in your life that will be affected by your laying down your life to honor God?

David M. Edwards is a man driven—driven by a passion to see people enter into the presence of God and driven to see, and be a part of, a new generation of seekers, those who seek the face of God and not just the "hands" of God. Many life experiences have shaped David into the teacher/writer/pastor/worshiper he is today. His music and teaching ministry takes him to places as far away as France, Germany, Switzerland, Romania, Ecuador, and the United Kingdom, as well as all over America.

David and his wife, Susan, and their three children have been in ministry for seventeen years. During this time, new songs of worship have been pouring out of him. David has worked with prolific songwriters and artists, such as Margaret Becker, Ginny Owens, Chris Eaton, Steve Hindalong, Greg Nelson, Natalie Grant, Kathy Troccoli, Matt Brouwer, Caleb Quaye, John Hartley, and Regi Stone. Many artists have recorded his songs.

When David describes his songs, he says, "These songs are all about God. They're not about me. Pain and life teach us to worship and cling to God, so my songs come from personal experiences of joy and pain in my own life. There's always something we can be grateful for, to come to God and thank Him."

In 2005 David was awarded *Worship Leader* magazine's "Best Scripture Song" Praise Award for his song "Create in Me," and in 2007 he received a *Worship Leader* magazine's Praise Award for his song "Holy Rain." His *Holy Rain* album with Regi Stone was released in 2007. For nine years in a row, David has been a winner of ASCAP's Popular Award Panel's recognition.

In 2003 David began his *Worship 365: Power to Worship Encounters*—a seminar where attendees not only learn about the basics of worship but experience God's presence as well. His critically acclaimed book in 2006, *Worship 365: The Power of a Worshiping Life*, developed out of the overwhelmingly positive response to these seminars. David's desire is for people to be ministered to as well as to perfect their craft and calling.

David's other books on worship include the Faithfully Yours: Psalms series—*Create in Me*, *Enter His Gates*, and *As High as the Heavens* (three books with worship CDs included); and the Worship through the Seasons with God series—*Season of Provision (Harvest)*, *Season of Promise (Advent)*, *Season of Passion (Easter)*, and *Season of Power (Pentecost)* (four books with worship CDs included). ·

David is general editor of the *Holman CSB Personal Worship Bible*.

In 2006 David became an official spokesman for the Bible League, which is one of the world's largest evangelical, nondenominational Scripture placement agencies. It provides Bibles and Bible studies to local churches in more than fifty countries, training and equipping Christians to use the Bible to make disciples and establish new churches that bring people into fellowship with Christ and His church. Also in 2006 David was appointed managing editor of *Worship Leader* magazine's *The Worshiper.*

To find out more about David Edwards's music, books, and ministry, contact:

Glenda McNalley
The Select Artist Group
P.O. Box 1418
LaVergne, TN 37086
www.theselectartistgroup.com
or
www.davidmedwards.com